Shipwrecks Along The Great Ocean Road

JACK LONEY

TENTH EDITION

First Edition 1967
Reprinted and Enlarged 1969
Revised and Enlarged 1973
Reprinted with Additions 1974
Further Revised 1975
Reprinted with Further Additions 1976
Reprinted 1979
Reprinted 1983
Reprinted 1988
Reprinted with Corrections 1993
Reprinted 1996
Reprinted 2003

**SHIPWRECKS ON THE VICTORIAN WEST COAST
FROM POINT LONSDALE TO PORTLAND**

ISBN 9599853 8 7

Acknowledgements

The support accorded the following publications has encouraged me to completely revise and enlarge this work dealing with shipping disasters along Victoria's western coastline and it has been compiled from early newspapers, diaries, books, reports of Marine Courts of Inquiry and a variety of official records.

Books used have been; **Wrecks Around Cape Otway, Shipwrecks Along the Great Ocean Road, Wrecks on Victoria's South West Coast**.

I also thank the following for their assistance; Marine Board of Victoria, Department of Shipping and Transport, La Trobe Library, Melbourne, Stan McPhee, Warrnambool.

The photographs of lithographs of H.M.S. SAPPHO and the clipper SCHOMBERG have been provided by the National Maritime Museum, Greenwich, London, England.

Jack Loney

Preface to the Tenth Edition

This book first appeared in 1967 under the title of "Wrecks Around Cape Otway" and now with sales exceeding 50,000 it has become my best selling shipwreck book.

The task of correcting and updating it over the past 25 years has been an interesting challenge and I thank my diving friends, fellow historians and interested readers who drew my attention to errors and provided additional information.

Some faint memories of those days when ships were lost are still to be found up and down the Great Ocean Road. A gravestone on some lonely headland, a few rotting jetty piles in a quiet little inlet, or faded photographs and mouldering relics in local museums – these still survive from that period of our history which is so near to our own times and yet in many ways so infinitely remote.

Jack Loney,
1993

Contents

In Text Illustrations

Centre Section Illustrations

MAHOGANY SHIP
H.M.S. SAPPHO
Remains of schooner OTWAY
MARIE GABRIELLE anchors
Schooner ENTERPRISE
Tom Pearce
Eva Carmichael
Captain Gibb
Ship ERIC THE RED
Ship JOSEPH H. SCAMMELL
Barquentine LA BELLA
Barque GLANEUSE
Barque EDINBURGH CASTLE
Grave at GODFREY wreck

Barque GEORGE ROPER
Barque NEWFIELD
W.B. GODFREY memorial
Clipper PAUL JONES
Barque FIJI
Barque HOLYHEAD
Barque INVERLOCHY
Barque FALLS OF HALLADALE
Barquentine SPECULANT
Survivors from WOLLOMAI
S.S. CASINO
M.V. CITY OF RAYVILLE
S.S. ORUNGAL

Maps

DIVERS, SHIPWRECKS ON THE VICTORIAN
WEST COAST ARE PROTECTED
UNDER COMMONWEALTH AND STATE
HISTORIC SHIPWRECKS LEGISLATION

Foreword

Although many fine ships were lost along Victoria's western coastline soon after the Hentys settled at Portland in 1834, evidence suggests a number of unidentified wrecks many years earlier.

The most fascinating wreck, the "MAHOGANY SHIP" is supposed to still lie hidden under sand between Port Fairy and Warrnambool, but further to the east heavy seas along the wild precipitous coastline soon destroyed the remains of other early disasters.

Last century settlers made some interesting discoveries. In the forties, a farmer sinking a well near Portland discovered a bunch of keys many feet underground and far from any habitation. A similar discovery was made at Limeburners' Point near Geelong, while an oar was unearthed near Point Lonsdale in 1851. Remains of cannon were also found near Warrnambool and a ship's boat of unknown origin lay in the sand at Skenes Creek for many years. All of these relics have long been decayed or lost.

Settlement at Portland, Port Fairy and Warrnambool stimulated sea trade with ports in northern Tasmania and later Port Phillip, and this brought a big increase in wrecks along a coast lacking safe anchorages in all weathers. Usually, small craft obtained some shelter west of Cape Otway when the easterlies struck, while Apollo and Loutit Bays provided reasonable protection from the south-westerly gales.

The discovery of gold soon brought the big clippers to Melbourne, their first Australian landfall after leaving Cape Town invariably being Cape Otway at the western entrance to Bass Strait. King Island divides this entrance into two channels. The southern channel, littered with reefs, forced mariners to choose the northern passage less than 50 miles in width. As there were no lights on King Island until 1861, ships hugged the Victorian coast anxiously seeking the Otway light, which had been completed in 1848.

The standard of navigation on most sailing ships was usually very poor and many ships approaching Melbourne from the west were often more than 50 miles away from their calculated position. Also, in bad weather, rain, fog, or calm, the crews often had little or no control over their ships. Now, modern navigational aids and reliable propulsion have effectively removed most hazards.

1 - Ships

Vessels having three or more masts, all square rigged. Clippers, the ultimate in ship construction, were rigged with additional sails and had more streamlined hulls. Their cargo carrying capacity was reduced, but this was offset by greater speed.

SACRAMENTO – 1853

Built 1850. 447 tons burthen.

News of the gold discoveries brought such an enormous influx of emigrants that countless ships were pressed into the Australian trade. The earliest lines trading to the colony placed orders in English and American shipyards for ships capable of accommodating hundreds of passengers and eventually names like MARCO POLO, JAMES BAINES, DONALD MACKAY, LIGHTNING, THERMOPYLAE and TORRENS became well known all over the world.

The ship SACRAMENTO, Captain W. Holmes master, inward bound from London with more than 300 passengers and crew, sighted land on April 26th, 1853 and was hove to at 9 p.m. that evening intending to enter Port Phillip early next morning.

Captain Holmes retired at midnight, leaving the Second Mate, James Donohue, in charge. At 2 a.m. the helmsman called his attention to the fact that the ship was apparently drifting towards the shore but no attempt was made to wear her. At 3 a.m. the captain was called out but it was then too late to save her, and within ten minutes she struck the Point Lonsdale Reef.

All on board were safely landed and taken in drays to Queenscliff, where they were treated with great kindness by Mrs Dod, wife of an early settler, until the steamer APHRASIA arrived to take them to Melbourne.

The ship's masts went overboard 24 hours after she struck, and in less than a week the hull broke in two, littering the beach between Point Lonsdale and Queenscliff with wreckage.

Just before the ship broke up Captain Holmes, the carpenter and Pilot Mansfield went on board and recovered 12 boxes of coin valued at about £60,000. This was taken to Melbourne on the Government schooner EMPIRE.

The Captain and Second Mate were both charged with neglect of duty. Captain Holmes was committed for trial and bail with three sureties of £500. Each was granted. However, at the next meeting of the Court all the witnesses had disappeared so the case ended. The Second Mate was sentenced to four months hard labour but mercy was recommended on account of his previous good conduct.

EARL OF CHARLEMONT – 1853

Built at Saint John, New Brunswick, Canada, in 1849. Two decks, a poop, three masts, square stern, no galleries. Figurehead of a man. Burthen 883 tons. Length, 147.8 feet; beam, 30.6 feet; depth, 22.7 feet.

6

Inward bound from Liverpool in charge of Captain William Garner with 435 emigrants and a cargo of coal, iron and general merchandise, the EARL OF CHARLEMONT passed Cape Otway about mid-afternoon on Friday, June 17th, 1853, sailing at about four knots.

At dusk she hove to in wet squally weather and remained a few miles offshore until 11 p.m., when the order was given to wear ship and steer south to south-east until 3 a.m. when the course was changed to west-north-west.

No land was visible and Captain Garner supposed the ship had drifted to about eight miles offshore while hove to. The same course was maintained until 4.30 a.m. when she wore up for the Heads, then believed to be about 15 miles off. About 20 minutes later, in heavy fog, she was found to be in breakers. The helm was immediately put hard to port but the ship struck heavily on the reef and within ten minutes the wheel was carried away and the foremast smashed.

At daylight the foremast stump and rigging were cut away to lighten the ship up forward and get her on to the beach; then the main topmast rigging and back stays followed, leaving the main yard to get the boats out. However, the vessel fell on her starboard, where the rising tide made a clean breach over her. Three boats were launched in an attempt to get a line to shore but all capsized, leaving their crews to struggle ashore. Other members of the crew clambered down the chains, along the fallen mast, then swam ashore. Mr Savage, a steerage passenger, also swam ashore with a line from the jib-boom enabling a strong rope to be attached between the wreck and beach. Then, an undamaged lifeboat was slung to the rope by the bow and stern like a cradle, enabling the passengers to land – ladies and children first, then the invalids, married men, single men, and last of all the captain.

By 8.30 in the evening all were safely ashore with the exception of a passenger named Robert Thwaites, who died from shock soon after the vessel struck. His body was eventually recovered from the wreck by his son and interred on The Bluff near where the ship struck.

Fires were lighted, food brought ashore, some sheep and a bullock from nearby McVean's Station killed, then all camped on the beach overnight.

When news of the wreck reached Geelong, Captain Ferguson, the Harbour Master, with Lloyd's surveyor proceeded to the scene aboard the Pilot Schooner ANONYMA with a supply of food, but, finding the sea too rough, returned to Queenscliff. Then, a plan to convey the stores by land was also abandoned when it was found no boat was available for crossing the river at Ocean Grove.

On the Monday following the wreck the Second Mate of the BOOMERANG reported that on arriving at the wreck on the previous morning he found the passengers and crew preparing to make their way to Geelong on eight bullock drays despatched by Mr Cowie, the Mayor of Geelong.

On Saturday evening, June 25th, a concert was arranged in the Theatre Royal, Malop Street, Geelong, for the benefit of passengers who had lost all of their possessions. Prices of admission were: Boxes 5/-, pit 2/6.

The ship and cargo were sold at auction on June 27th to Mr William Burrows for £900 and the boats as they lay on the beach brought £25.

Soon after, Captain Garner left for England on the MADAGASCAR but when she disappeared without trace ugly rumours circulated concerning her fate. She carried £25,000 in gold and the authorities were never certain whether she had been seized by pirates who had shipped aboard and murdered the passengers.

The Board of Inquiry investigating the wreck came under severe criticism when, after collecting evidence which proved carelessness on the part of the captain and his officers, and doubtful treatment of the immigrants, issued a report but took no further action. According to the press the captain seemed indifferent to the dangerous course of the CHARLEMONT and the ship was poorly conducted throughout the voyage. Provisions were bad, the interior filthy and a regular trade was carried on in spirits, porter and ale which kept passengers in a state of constant riot and disorder.

NEW ZEALANDER – 1853

Built in 1852. 1309 tons. Registered at Liverpool.

Fire destroyed this emigrant ship as she lay at anchor in Portland Bay on the night of December 16th, 1853.

The fire broke out at about 4 a.m. and within an hour the ship was completely enveloped in flames from stem to stern, burning the hull to the waterline. Nobody could approach the ship but fortunately she was anchored well away from all other ships and the light breeze was off-shore. At about 5 a.m. the main mast went over the side but the ship continued to burn throughout most of the next day.

In the afternoon, the Harbour Master, Captain Fawthrop, and a party succeeded in cutting her anchor cables and towing her to the beach off Whalers' Bluff where she continued to burn.

At the subsequent investigation, Captain Brown said he believed the fire had originated in her cargo of 450 tons of coal. When the fire broke out the only persons on board were three officers, four sailors and a boy. Eighteen of the crew were in gaol for refusing duty and all the immigrants had left some days before. The eighteen substitutes who had replaced the men in gaol, together with the officers and boy, were immediately taken into custody but were later cleared of suspicion and released.

SCHOMBERG – 1855

Built at Aberdeen, Scotland, in 1855. 2,284 tons gross. Length, 288 feet; beam, 45 feet; depth 29.2 feet.

Two years later the most scandalous wreck in Victoria's maritime history took place about a mile east of Curdie's Inlet, near where present-day Peterborough stands.

8

The Colonial clipper SCHOMBERG, built at a cost of £43,103, was expected to eclipse all previous sailing records between England and Australia recently established by the famous Black Ball Line ships MARCO POLO and LIGHTNING. She was a magnificent ship. Built of wood, she was heavily sparred with a lower main mast of pitch pine 110 feet long weighing 15 tons. Her main yard was a fantastic 113 feet in length; maintopsail yard 93 feet; top gallant yard 65 feet; royal yard 55 feet and skysail yard 45 feet. From her keel to her main mast truck measured more than 200 feet, while in favourable conditions she carried 18,000 square yards of sail. Her poop was 62 feet long and almost 9 feet high with its centre portion set aside as a dining saloon 20 feet wide fitted to accommodate 60 persons. Colours used here were gold and white with velvet pile carpets and mahogany furniture. There were many windows and ten large mirrors were spaced at intervals around the walls. The ladies' drawing room was inlaid with rosewood and included a sofa capable of seating 30 persons, while the ladies' saloon was decorated with birds-eye maple and mahogany. The chairs were covered with green, purple and gold satin damask with matching velvet carpets. A piano was provided. The library and writing room held about 400 books and was lined in oak. All three classes of cabins were well furnished and some first class accommodation included a bath. The galley could prepare food for 1000 people, a cow was carried for fresh milk and there were pens for fowls and pigs. In addition, she carried 90,000 gallons of water for drinking, domestic and fire-fighting purposes.

The SCHOMBERG was placed under the command of the Commodore of the line, Captain James Nicol "Bully" Forbes, previous commander of the clippers MARCO POLO and LIGHTNING. An Aberdonian, Forbes was a man of outstanding ability and nerve, but bragging and a quick temper marred his character and finally led to his downfall. His first command, an old brig considered by many to be totally unseaworthy, was outstandingly successful, gaining him many influential friends in shipping circles, and soon after he was placed in charge of vessels in the Australian trade. James Baines, founder of the famous Black Ball Line, always seemed very proud of his boastful Commodore.

Forbes, who described the SCHOMBERG as "the noblest ship that ever floated on water", was regarded as a devil at sea but a pious man ashore and the originator of the slogan, "Melbourne or Hell in 60 days".

It was rumoured that he cared little for the comfort of his passengers and often carried too much sail, causing his ship to be awash in brisk weather. This caused him to lose the fore topmast from the LIGHTNING off Cape Horn when racing her home from Australia in 1854.

The SCHOMBERG left England for Australia on her maiden voyage on 6th October, 1855, flying the signal, "Melbourne in Sixty Days", and despite some adverse weather, made reasonable time, her greatest speed being 15 knots and her best 24-hour run being 368 miles. At 1 p.m. on Christmas

Day, 79 days out, she was sighted off Cape Bridgewater but spent the next two days tacking against a strong wind.

At 9.15 p.m. on the evening of the disaster she was standing in towards land, close hauled on the starboard tack, with single reefed topsails, and reefed up gallant sails, heading north-west with lowlines hauled, and making five or six knots. Forbes was playing cards in the saloon when the Mate, Henry Keen, reported the ship close in to the shore, but Forbes, who was having mixed luck, decided to play another rubber before going on deck and giving the order to change tack. When he finally gave the order to "bout ship" it was too late as the wind had dropped and the vessel refused to "come round". Forbes next tried to "wear" her. The head sails were all aback, the jibs were close, the after yards braced, but the ship, embayed and caught in an inshore current, slid gently on to a reef near Curdie's Inlet about 35 miles west of Cape Otway. This reef is close to the inlet and extends from a rock about 17 feet high, joined to the shore by a narrow neck of sand, awash at high tide and constantly being changed by the action of the sea. It is now known as Schomberg Rock.

Forbes, on being told that his ship was hard aground, said angrily, "Let her go to Hell and tell me when she is on the beach," and again went below. When the SCHOMBERG struck in about 20 feet of water her head was facing out to sea so the sails were kept on for about an hour in the hope that the breeze would lift her off, but she did not move.

The mate then let go the starboard anchor and with the help of a passenger named Millar, safely disembarked the passengers aboard the West Coast steamer QUEEN, which hove in sight the following morning on her way from Warrnambool to Melbourne.

The wreck was then abandoned until Forbes and the agents boarded her on December 30th, leaving soon after considering it unsafe. An unusual vessel was chartered to attempt immediate recovery of the cargo. She was a Dutch galliot named ENGELKENS, more at home on the Zuyder Zee than the oceans of the world, and probably in Melbourne with a cargo of cheeses and Dutchmen bound for the goldfields. She sailed to the wreck but returned at once reporting the seas too dangerous for salvage work. About 130 persons camped on the beach opposite the wreck anticipating big hauls, but when the SCHOMBERG went to pieces on 6th January, scattering timbers for miles along the coast, little of real value was recovered. Most of the passengers' luggage had been taken off a few days earlier.

The remains were sold on 12th January for £447-9-0. The ship and cargo were insured for £30,000. A quantity of the cargo eventually drifted ashore where it was sold by auction along with portion of the wreck and 2,000 tons of rails originally meant for the Geelong to Melbourne railway to a Warrnambool syndicate for £65. S.S. QUEEN received £150 from the Black Ball Line for taking most of the 500 passengers on to Melbourne.

Two later attempts to recover cargo from the wreck failed. In 1864 six men were inspecting the wreck when a huge wave smashed their boat, drowning two of them. The following year another attempt was also unsuccessful.

A mass meeting of passengers at the Mechanics Institute, Melbourne, on January 3rd, 1856, passed the following resolutions:

1. Conduct of the Captain, surgeon and some officers was ungentlemanly, discourteous and grossly immoral.
2. It was not only a general impression of the passengers but certain knowledge of many that the loss of the ship was due to the negligence of the captain.
3. Contracts entered into between the owners and passengers were not fulfilled.
4. A deputation should be appointed to press for Government investigation into the loss of the SCHOMBERG.

Following the meeting the Passenger Act of 1855 was invoked for the first time and Lieutenant Pascoe was appointed to formally hear the complaints. However, so many of the witnesses contradicted each other that the magistrate dismissed all charges, considering them of a frivolous nature.

Captain Forbes was also committed for trial under the Merchant Shipping Act for neglect of duty on the following charges:

1. Not altering the course of the ship and thereby causing the destruction thereof.
2. Not keeping the ship from shore.
3. Not keeping diligent watch on deck.
4. Not having the anchor ready to let go in approaching the shore.
5. Not letting the anchor go to prevent the vessel striking the shore.
6. Standing too close to shore whereby the ship was destroyed.

Forbes was acquitted when it was proved that the boatswain Hodge had been bribed by a number of passengers to testify against him and controversy arose concerning the use of anchors to save the clipper.

Forbes was not given another major command with the Black Ball Line and died on June 4th, 1874, at the age of 52 after a few years in the China Seas. On his tombstone is carved, "Master of the Famous MARCO POLO".

TUBAL CAIN - 1862

Built at Liverpool 1851. 787 tons.

On the evening of August 26, 1862, while proceeding west with a cargo of coal and under the command of Captain Clarke, the iron-framed planked ship, TUBAL CAIN, collided with the ship CONSTANCE, 1,100 tons, about 200 miles west-south-west from Cape Otway.

The TUBAL CAIN sank immediately, drowning 12 members of her crew, including her captain. The only man saved was working in the rigging at the time of the collision and managed to leap on to the deck of the CONSTANCE.

The bows of the CONSTANCE were stove in and her deck was ripped up as far as the fore hatch. She lost her bowsprit, foremast, main and mizzen top gallant masts and cutwater but her pumps were able to control the water level. Canvas was stretched across the bows but the CONSTANCE shipped a considerable amount of water during two days of rough weather.

Captain Hewitt, master of the CONSTANCE, told a Court of Inquiry that his ship was sailing east just between daylight and dark when visibility is very poor. The sea was moderate but the sky very dark. Both crews were at tea when the ships collided. The TUBAL CAIN was on the starboard tack and the CONSTANCE on the port tack travelling at eight knots. She rammed the TUBAL CAIN near her fore rigging and dragged along her port side, ripping it out and sinking her almost immediately. As the vessel heeled over he saw a figure leap from the TUBAL CAIN's rigging on to the deck. A boat was immediately lowered but in the gathering gloom no trace of survivors was found although wreckage was scattered over a wide area.

The death of Captain Clarke, a popular and well-known figure in Melbourne shipping circles, caused wide regret. He was 70 years of age and had indicated his intention to retire soon after the fateful voyage.

LIGHT OF THE AGE – 1868

Clipper of 1287 tons. Built in 1855 and registered at Liverpool. Some references describe her as barque rigged.

Inward bound from Liverpool with 45 passengers and a general cargo of salt, slates, pipes, liquors and general cargo, the LIGHT OF THE AGE was totally wrecked about four miles east of Ocean Grove on January 16th, 1868.

Two days earlier she had sailed east along the Victorian coast with the DOVER CASTLE, but after rounding Cape Otway the weather deteriorated and contact was lost.

A lookout was kept for the pilot as she neared Port Phillip Heads but she missed stays and drifted ashore. Immediately she struck an anchor was dropped while rockets and cannon were fired. The wreck was eventually seen by the pilot schooner RIP through rain squalls, and a boat was sent off to confirm her grounding. The officer in charge returned to the pilot schooner about an hour later to report that the LIGHT OF THE AGE was bilged with about 15 feet of water in the hold and requiring immediate assistance.

Soon after, the masts fell and the vessel turned broadside on to the beach, but the RIP took off the passengers and most of the crew of 34 before returning to Melbourne, where the owners had made arrangements for their reception. The tugs WARHAWK, RESOLUTE and TITAN stood by but the ship broke up rapidly.

The schooners BEN BOLT, RESULT and PHOENIX carried out salvage operations for several weeks, the PHOENIX herself being wrecked near Point Lonsdale when returning with a load of salvaged goods.

The LIGHT OF THE AGE was valued at £5,000 and carried a cargo estimated to be worth £12,000.

The Steam Navigation Board Inquiry found as follows:
1. The ship carried obsolete charts and sailing directions, most dated about 1861. Revised charts were available each year and it was the responsibility of the owners and masters to acquire them.
2. No boats were available for rapid launching. When three members of the crew fell overboard during the voyage nothing could be done to save them.
3. The First Officer, Third Officer, boatswain, carpenter and sailmaker all gave evidence that the master, Captain Porter, was often drunk and incapable of command.
4. The Captain's calculations were often incorrect and the ship was off course on many occasions.

Captain Porter was found guilty of drunkenness; he neglected the navigation of his ship and was unfit to be in command. His certificate was cancelled.

VICTORIA TOWER – 1869

Built at Liverpool in 1869. 1,750 tons gross. Length, 247 feet; beam, 40.1 feet; depth, 23.7 feet.

On Sunday, 17th October, 1869, a report was received from Bream Creek that the ship, VICTORIA TOWER, inward bound from Liverpool, was ashore nearby.

The vessel, 85 days out and under the command of Captain Kerr, had run into dense fog soon after rounding Cape Otway and this had prevented an accurate estimate of her position. As a precaution her master had ordered rockets and flares fired at regular intervals.

She struck without warning, the force driving the mainmast through her keel and breaking her back. Anchors were let go immediately to hold her but she drove broadside on to the sea about 400 yards from the shore.

The pinnace was launched but the huge sea smashed it immediately, but a local resident, Mr Noble, who had seen the wreck, waited until a second boat containing six members of the crew reached shore, then hurried to Geelong for assistance.

The Geelong Harbour Master was unable to make telegraphic communication with Queenscliff but despatched a messenger on horseback with a request that the rocket gear be forwarded, then he and the Customs agent hurried to the wreck.

Most of the crew and 40 passengers were still on board but as the sea calmed all were landed, using the ship's boats and local fishing craft.

In calm weather luggage and ship's fittings were loaded on to the tug TITAN only a short time before rough seas reduced the ship to a total wreck.

The VICTORIA TOWER was worth £25,000 in addition to the cargo, but the hull and cargo were auctioned for £6,000. In calm weather, most of the cargo of iron pipes, bottled beer, hardware, salt and slates was salvaged.

An Inquiry conducted by the Steam Navigation Board on October 27th, found Captain Kerr had erred in not hauling the ship to the south-east on a starboard tack immediately he doubted his position, and not casting the lead to ascertain the depth of water. They suspended his certificate for six months.

SUSSEX - 1871

Built at Glasgow, 1853. 1,305 tons gross. Length, 230 feet; beam, 32.2 feet; depth 22 feet.

The wooden ship SUSSEX left Plymouth on October 9th, 1871, for Melbourne in command of Captain Collard with a general cargo, 47 passengers and a crew of 47. It was Captain Collard's fourth voyage to Melbourne and the ship's twenty-eighth.

The voyage out was uneventful and after the ship rounded Cape Otway the passengers presented a testimonial to the captain in acknowledgment of his skill and kindness.

On December 31st the ship, running before the wind, arrived within sight of Port Phillip Heads and all were looking forward to spending New Year's Day in Melbourne. As evening approached a keen watch was kept for the Queenscliff lights, but apparently a light seen was mistaken for Cape Schanck, the ship's course changed and the mistake discovered too late. When breakers were seen ahead an attempt was made to bring the ship to, but it was too late, and at 9 p.m. she ran on to a reef one and a half miles west of Barwon Heads and 100 yards to the eastward of the remains of the steamer ANT, wrecked five years earlier.

Immediately the ship struck blue lights and rockets were fired to attract attention and all passengers were warned to prepare to abandon her. The seas drove her over the rocks on to sand before a boat manned by Third Officer O'Flaherty with a crew of six volunteers launched a boat in an attempt to get help from the pilot cutter at Queenscliff. They cleared the ship and succeeded in rounding The Bluff, but, when attempting to land the boat was swamped, drowning all occupants except a seaman named Labton. A sea struck the stern of the boat, driving it broadside on to the surf, and before the bow could be brought around, another wave capsized it, trapping the men underneath. They managed to swim clear, then clung on to the keel until washed off one by one. Labton, a strong swimmer, reached the shore but the others were not seen alive again. Three bodies were washed ashore and the boat was recovered near the wreck.

Meanwhile, the signals of distress were seen by local residents and a farmer named Angus from Barwon Heads hurried to the wreck, lit a fire and remained on watch until a neighbour arrived. Then he rode into Geelong to report the wreck to the Superintendent of Police, Mr Bookey, and word was sent to Melbourne and Queenscliff.

Nothing could be done from the shore as the sea was sweeping over the ship, which was lying stern to the beach with a slight list to port, her lower fore and main topsails set, her stunsail booms rigged out but standing very steady.

The tug WARHAWK soon arrived from Queenscliff where she had been anchored and arrangements were quickly made to transfer passengers and crew, using a dinghy and one of the ship's boats. Other vessels quickly on the scene included the paddle tugs TITAN and CHALLENGE, tug MYSTERY and the Queenscliff lifeboat.

The captain saved the ship's papers, the crew their kits, while later, most of the passengers' luggage was salvaged almost undamaged. Mr Lane, the Collector of Customs at Geelong, arranged for police to camp on the beach to discourage looting.

An inquiry commenced on January 2nd, 1872, and the court found that Captain Collard was responsible for the loss of the ship. They stated that he should have verified that the light first seen on the starboard bow was not Cape Schanck, and also he should not have steered for the light on the port bow after discovering that his assumed position showed an error in the steering of the ship. His certificate was suspended for six months.

The ship was valued at £10,000, while the cargo, consisting mainly of softgoods and oilman's stores, was estimated to be worth more than £44,000. At an auction held on the beach on January 4th, ship and cargo were sold to a syndicate of Geelong merchants for £6,800. A wire rope from the foremast to the beach was used for hauling boats loaded with cargo to and fro, the boats being towed into shallow water by a team of 12 bullocks, and an iron tramway was laid down the sandhill to haul the goods from the beach to drays which carried them to the Customs shed at Geelong, where they were sold by auction. Proceeds reached £20,000, including £10-10-0 for a grand piano which was valued at £250. After paying all expenses the syndicate made a profit of £11,900, or £700 per share.

Lighters and rafts also loaded large quantities of goods for Melbourne. One airtight raft, constructed on the beach, was destroyed on its first trip. An iron tank raft, capable of carrying about 30 tons, proved more successful. Another method was to drop cases over the side to be washed ashore when the tide was setting in that direction. Six trunks of boots were found washed up between Barwon Heads and Queenscliff and others were found at Portarlington and Werribee.

Included in the cargo was a quantity of furniture valued at £1,200, belonging to Mr Josiah Austin. Also, a cow carried on board for fresh milk was eventually slaughtered by a local butcher, two sheep were landed still in good health and the ship's dog swam ashore.

LOCH ARD - 1878

Built in Glasgow, Scotland, 1873. 1,693 tons gross. Length, 263.7 feet; beam, 38.3 feet; depth, 23 feet.

Lonely and deserted until recently, Glenample Station homestead stands a short distance off the Great Ocean Road a few miles west of Princetown, a pathetic reminder of a tragedy which struck deeply into the hearts of the colonists a century ago when the smart iron clipper LOCH ARD met her doom on the rocks below precipitous Mutton Bird Island.

Owned by the Glasgow Shipping Company, the LOCH ARD was twice dismasted on her maiden voyage but was considered to be a fast, comfortable ship. Her two best passages carrying wool home from Australia were: Melbourne to London in 93 days and Melbourne to Dungeness in 93 days.

The LOCH ARD left Gravesend for Melbourne on March 1st, 1878 with 54 passengers and crew together with a general cargo valued at more than £53,000. The voyage out was uneventful and on the night of May 31st her master, Captain Gibb, believed her to be many miles off the Victorian coast, although a man was sent aloft to watch for the Otway light.

In fact, the ship was close inshore near the mouth of Sherbrooke Creek and off one of the wildest coastlines in the world. In the early hours of the morning the coastal haze lifted and revealed rugged cliffs only a short distance away. More sail was set in a desperate effort to clear the shore, but before the vessel could respond she was in breakers. Anchors were let go but they dragged on the sandy bottom so an attempt was made to place her on the port tack. The anchors were slipped, and just when it seemed she would clear the perpendicular cliffs of an island, she struck a ledge on her starboard quarter and began to sink. As she rolled her yards struck high on the cliff, dislodging rocks and showering the passengers and crew with spars and rigging.

An attempt was made to launch the port lifeboat but the six men it contained were thrown into the sea when a huge wave capsized it. One of these, an apprentice named Tom Pearce, was trapped under the boat for some time, but after he dived out from beneath it he clung to its side for nearly three hours before it was eventually washed into a forbidding looking gorge about 100 yards from where the ship had sunk. Leaving the boat, he swam through the surf to a small sandy beach and was resting there when he heard a weak cry and saw a woman drifting towards shore on a spar.

Among the passengers on the ship was Doctor Emery Carmichael, his wife, four daughters and two sons. When the ship sank, one daughter, Eva, seized a floating hen coop and was joined by Messrs Jones and Mitchell.

Later, when all three attempted to swim to a nearby spar, Eva reached it but the two men disappeared. She was then carried into the gorge where her weak cries attracted Pearce, who swam out and brought her ashore.

Pearce was reasonably well attired, but Miss Carmichael, clad only in a nightdress, was semi-conscious and suffered from the cold. After helping her to a cave at the western end of the gorge, Pearce returned to the beach to search for more survivors but found no one. Among the wreckage he discovered a case of brandy and, breaking open the top, took a long drink before returning to Miss Carmichael, who drank the remainder.

After a short sleep, Pearce left her in the cave and climbed the perpendicular cliffs. Following a track, he met by chance G. Ford and W. Till, employees of Messrs Gibson and McArthur of Glenample Station, who were mustering sheep. After gasping out his story, Pearce returned to the gorge while the two men rode to the station for assistance. When they returned it was getting dark and Miss Carmichael had disappeared, but after a long search she was found crouching under some bushes shivering with cold and fear, believing their calls to be those of aborigines.

Carefully she was raised to the top of the cliff and taken to Glenample homestead, where she remained for some time before going on to Melbourne.

In Melbourne, Pearce was hailed as a hero! The Governor, Sir George Bowen, presented him with an inscribed gold watch and chain, also a locket on behalf of the Government of Victoria. The presentation took place in the Melbourne Town Hall before a gathering of 5,000 people. The people of Warrnambool collected a sum of money for him and presented him with gifts while a committee in Sydney recognized his bravery with a set of navigation instruments. He also received the first gold medal struck by the Royal Humane Society of Victoria.

Only five bodies were recovered from the wreck, two of these being Miss Carmichael's mother and a sister. Four of the bodies were buried on top of the cliff and the fifth was buried in the sand on High Cliff Beach where it was discovered. When the bodies were being recovered a small raft was constructed and a settler named Cowley was lowered by a rope to keep it off the rocks during the raising operations.

A quantity of cargo came ashore and was stacked inside the gorge above what was believed to be the high water mark. Charles Macgillivray, a local settler, was placed in charge of salvaged goods until the Customs arrived. His advice to move all cargo to high ground was not heeded and, during a storm, most was washed out to sea and lost.

Three Geelong men, Haworth, Miller and Matthews, successfully bid £2,120 for the remains of the ship and her cargo but recovered only a small amount and lost the steamer NAPIER when she ran ashore in Port Campbell Bay.

For many years the exact whereabouts of the LOCH ARD were lost, but in 1967 a Warrnambool skin diver, Stan McPhee, using a launch and light aircraft, located the wreck near where she had been reported lost.

He immediately placed questions regarding her ownership into legal hands but meanwhile, skin divers and abalone fishermen who had watched his movements from nearby cliffs began stripping the remains. Small charges of gelignite were used to blow holes in the hull, until Commonwealth Police moved in early in 1969 and took possession of more than 50 tons of lead, copper and bronze from homes and properties at Cobden, Port Campbell, Peterborough, Timboon and Geelong. However, many tons of metal had already been smuggled out of the district and sold. Following charges arising from illegal salvaging several persons were fined, while the Receiver of Wrecks held all salvage pending the establishment of a legal owner of the wreck.

But what of the two survivors? Tom Pearce returned to the sea and did not meet Eva Carmichael again. His next vessel, the LOCH SUNART, was wrecked off the Irish coast in 1879 but once again he reached safety. Later he joined the Royal Mail Steamship Company, where he rose to the rank of captain. He married the sister of one of the apprentices who lost his life on the LOCH ARD and his two sons saw service at sea. Tom (Junior) lost his life when the LOCH VENNACHAR disappeared off Kangaroo Island in 1905 and his other son, Robert, was lost during World War 2 when a ship under his command was bombed and sunk while in a convey bound for Malta. Ill-health forced Tom Pearce's retirement in 1908 and he died in December of the same year.

Eva Carmichael remained at Glenample for more than a month before travelling to Melbourne where she remained until she sailed for home on S.S. TANJORE late in August. She married Mr T. Townsend and lived in Bedford, England, where she died in 1934. She had three sons, all of whom married.

ERIC THE RED – 1880

Built in Bath, Maine, U.S.A. in 1871. Reconditioned 1879. 1,580 tons gross. Length, 198.7 feet; beam, 41.1 feet; depth, 17.5 feet.

The year 1880 was an important one for the rapidly expanding city of Melbourne, busy preparing for its first International Exhibition which had attracted exhibits from all the leading manufacturing countries of the world.

The wooden ship ERIC THE RED, commissioned by American trade representatives, left New York on June 12th, 1880, for Melbourne, loaded with exhibits, two passengers and a crew of 25.

At noon on Friday, September 3rd, 84 days out, the ship was making ten knots in clear weather and expected to pick up the Otway light early in the evening. When darkness fell Captain Allen posted a watch aloft and climbed into the rigging himself on several occasions before the light was seen in the early hours of the morning. The ship was then travelling at eight knots with almost full sail set, the weather at sea being clear with a slight swell although a heavy land haze made visibility poor.

Believing the ship to be at least six miles off Cape Otway, Captain Allen steered towards the light but he had badly misjudged his position and the vessel struck the Otway Reef, which extends about two miles out to sea in a south-easterly direction from the lighthouse.

When the ship struck the captain ordered the helm to be put hard up, thinking she might float off, but a heavy sea broke over the quarter deck, carrying away the steering gear. As she swung around with her stern to the south, she shipped a tremendous sea which swept everything before it. One roller snapped the mizzentopmast; the next broke the ship amidships, with the main mast going over the side. The foremast went with the fore part of the deck house, carrying three crewmen and the long boat which was the vessel which plunged bow first into deep water. The forward section stove in at the bows, drifted away. The men were eventually able to launch the damaged boat and keep it afloat.

The captain, second mate and others clung to the mizzen mast which then fell into the sea, taking them with it. Sewell, the owner's son, was washed off, but succeeded in holding on to a kerosene case from which he was picked up later. Those drowned were H. Ackman, steward; G. de Silver, sailor; G. Daghlyne, carpenter; and J. Vaughan, passenger; who must have gone down when the vessel struck, as they were not seen again.

Fortunately, the small coastal steamer DAWN, commanded by Captain Jones, was returning to Warrnambool from Melbourne and was about six miles off Cape Otway when faint cries of distress were heard by the crew.

The DAWN was stopped, boats were lowered, and rockets and blue lights fired to attract the attention of the survivors. Soon after, the partly swamped long boat was recovered and the difficult rescue of 17 survivors, including the captain, was made from a large portion of the side and bow of the ship shortly before it was thrown on to rocks at Point Franklin about two miles east of Cape Otway.

Captain Jones spent several hours searching for survivors without success, and soon after dawn signalled the lighthouse with news of the disaster, which was immediately telegraphed to Melbourne. As soon as possible search parties combed the beaches to the east and west.

All that remained of the ship was a large piece of wreckage awash on the north-east corner of the reef. An immense quantity of wreckage floated on to Point Franklin. This point is low and the beach was covered with debris piled several feet high, kerosene tins and beautiful red pine timber being the most prominent objects. One whole side of the ship lay on the rocks with the copper sheathing stripped off in several places, together with portion of a mast still carrying a large piece of canvas. Some of the goods salvaged here included kegs of nails, sewing machines, rolls of wire, bicycles, clocks, axe and scythe handles, Bibles, croquet balls, croquet mallets, rat traps and fly wheels, while a little further to the east more boxes of sewing machines, crates of sarsaparilla, chairs, a sailor's chest and a host of smaller items floated ashore. More wreckage was picked up at Apollo Bay, Western Port, Port Campbell and Peterborough.

The Government steamers PHAROS and VICTORIA left Melbourne soon after the wreck to clear the sailing lanes and the PHAROS discovered the first large piece of wreckage near the Henty Reef south of Apollo Bay. Closer examination showed it to be a deckhouse containing chairs, timber boxes, a ladder and a variety of small articles. A boat was lowered and it was towed into a small bay between Storm Point and Point Bunbury to be anchored about 40 yards off shore. The VICTORIA and the steamer OTWAY, bound from Adelaide to Melbourne, also recovered wreckage.

Several residents at Apollo Bay rebuilt their homes with timber salvaged from the wreck. The Cawood family constructed elaborate extensions to their well-known guest house, Milford House, and a Mr Burgess used timbers to construct a ketch he named APOLLO.

Only one body was recovered and buried in the Otway cemetery about a mile north from the lighthouse.

The Mayor and Town Clerk of Warrnambool boarded the DAWN on her arrival and offered hospitality to the survivors. Three of the crew were sent to hospital while the remainder stayed at the Olive Branch Hotel before returning to Melbourne.

No inquiry was held by the Victorian Government but in July, 1881, costly presents were awarded to Captain Jones and his men by the United States Government, who thanked them for the "prompt, persevering and seamanlike qualities displayed by him, his officers and crew in rescuing the survivors". Then, the Victorian Government presented Captain Allen with £25; every penny of which he distributed among Melbourne and local Warrnambool charities; £15 to S. Poats, Chief Mate; and £5 each to seamen Dave, Lear, Stead, Jager, Edwards, Hammond, Black and Hanson.

In 1881 a red warning light was installed at the base of the lighthouse almost 300 feet above sea level to warn vessels approaching close to the reef. The light was not seen at sea until the ship was about three miles off and it was to prove an effective safeguard for more than 80 years.

Visitors to the lighthouse may clearly see the reef where ERIC THE RED struck and those who venture on to the small, almost inaccessible beaches nearby, find pieces of wreckage in rock pools and among the sand dunes. One of the ship's anchors which lay deeply embedded in rocks on the eastern side of Point Franklin may now be inspected in the lighthouse reserve.

PAUL JONES – 1886

Built at Portsmouth, New Haven, U.S.A., 1877. 1,258 tons gross. Length, 221.4 feet; beam, 41.2 feet; depth, 24.6 feet.

The American clipper PAUL JONES excited great admiration during her first visit to Melbourne late in 1885.

Built for the trade with China and the Dutch East Indies, her hollow lines forward earned her the nickname "Razor Face". Great things were expected from her but at no time did she turn in outstanding sailing performances.

When her cargo was being unloaded in Melbourne her main yard was broken, and following an inquiry the Port Melbourne Stevedore Company and her master, Captain Winn, were ordered to share the cost of its replacement.

No cargo was available for loading and during the delay Captain Winn paid off all the crew except the mate. When she left Melbourne in ballast on March 19th, 1886, few of the original crew had again signed on.

In fact, Captain Winn had considerable difficulty signing a crew as it seems the PAUL JONES was considered a "hell ship" by many seamen. When he did finally round up a crew of near "dead beats" and "no hopers" what a cosmopolitan group they were! There were four Americans, four Germans, three Scotsmen, three Finns, two Swedes, also a Frenchman, Irishman, Norwegian, Brazilian, Englishman and Dane.

When only a few miles outside Port Phillip Heads off Lorne, a wisp of smoke was seen near the stern. Captain Winn ordered a hatch removed for inspection but immediately this was done the whole stern burst into flames against which buckets and pumps proved totally ineffective. The fire gradually gained control, and as the rigging on the mizzen mast caught alight, the heat became so intense that all but the Captain and Mate were ordered to the boats.

Hundreds of sightseers at Lorne, attracted by the billowing clouds of black smoke, climbed hills around the town to witness the end of the ship.

The British ship ANTIOPE rescued the crew, while the LIGURIA and NELSON stood by to offer help. The Captain and Mate were finally forced to abandon the ship several hours after the outbreak and eventually all were landed at Port Melbourne.

The Government steamer DESPATCH, sent to sink the hulk, found it floating but burnt almost to the water-line about six miles off Lorne. A hole was cut in the side and it sank two hours later, leaving a considerable amount of wreckage floating over a wide area. Fears were expressed that some of the larger pieces would be a hazard for shipping and vessels were warned to avoid the area. Most of the crew had time to save their effects but the Captain lost everything. A considerable amount of charred wreckage floated ashore over a wide area during the next week but the only items of any value recovered were the boats used by the crew when they left the ship. These brought £29-7-6 at auction in Melbourne.

JOSEPH H. SCAMMELL – 1891

Built at Eatonville, Nova Scotia, 1884. Named after a New York merchant. 1410 tons. Length, 223 feet; beam, 39.2 feet; depth, 22.5 feet.

The destruction of the American ship JOSEPH H. SCAMMELL on a reef near Point Danger, Torquay, on Thursday night, May 7th, 1891 sparked off a wave of smuggling and pilfering without parallel in the Geelong district.

She left New York on January 13th and set sail for Melbourne under Captain Chapman, who also had most of his money invested in the voyage. The complement of 22 included his wife, daughter and a stewardess.

Shortly after sailing the ship encountered adverse winds, only varied occasionally with fine weather until the Cape of Good Hope was reached. Then good headway was made with day runs reaching 300 miles until Australian waters were entered, when thick showers and heavy squalls lashed the ship.

On the one hundred and fourteenth day out Cape Otway was sighted and a course set for Port Phillip Heads. About an hour after sighting the entrance more squalls blew up from the south, forcing the ship to tack under short canvas while she flew the pilot flag signal. The coastline was misty and uncertain but Captain Chapman expected to take on a pilot early in the morning and pass through the Heads. As darkness fell he picked up what he believed were the lights at Queenscliff, also the Cape Schanck light and another light on Arthur's Seat. Although he believed the ship to be on a true course each time a new one was set she was apparently forced inshore by a strong current and in the darkness struck a reef with a force that sent a violent tremor through every timber. She then commenced to bump heavily, pounding against the reef throughout the night, rising and falling with the breakers like a log. Those on board spent a terrifying night holding on to the cabin railings expecting to be crushed by falling spars and swept out into the sea.

A local fisherman, Felix Rosser, was the first to notice the ship in danger when he returned home after attending to some crayfish pots in Zealy Bay. He saw a dark mass loom close to the shore and had remarked to his wife that a ship was in far too close when he saw her signals of distress. In the stormy conditions there was little he could do but at about 2 a.m. when the sea had abated he put off his fishing boat and rowed to within about 300 yards of the ship, but the surf prevented him approaching closer. Returning, he lit a fire on the beach and remained on watch throughout the night while word was sent to Geelong.

At daylight he again pulled out to the wreck and at about the same time a boat containing three men was lowered. It broke away from the davits as it touched the sea and was forced ashore. Later in the morning it returned to the ship and eventually succeeded in landing the entire crew, who were taken to Follett's Coffee Palace.

At about mid-day the ship began to break up. First, the top gallant mast was carried away, and later in the afternoon the upper section of the other masts fell, bringing down the rigging. The small sail the ship carried when she went ashore was soon torn to ribbons and by dusk the foremast was leaning over the side. Captain Chapman, fearing that the ship would break up, refused to allow the crew to return on board to recover personal belongings. Late in the evening the hull appeared badly strained and when daylight came all that was to be seen was a shapeless mass of timber. Wreckage and cargo littered the beaches for miles, and Mr P. Holden, the Geelong Customs officer, three mounted police and several constables set up a camp on the beach to prevent looting.

Those who visited the wreck two days later found her a total loss. The remains of the hull had canted over to the weather side, releasing hundreds of articles of cargo which floated in with the tide. Great rolls of printing paper, saturated with salt water and reduced back to pulp, were lying high up on the beach or embedded in the sand. Packages of machinery were widely scattered, and the shore for miles was fringed with hundreds of battered and punctured tins of kerosene. Sections of decking were lying on the sand and nearby lay the lower half of the main mast and a few spars. Close by the police camp lay the stern with the words "Joseph H. Scammell, St. John N.B." carved in gilt letters. Tobacco was lying everywhere but most of it was saturated with kerosene.

By mid-day on Sunday, three days after the wreck, more than 2000 spectators had gathered but there were now two Customs officers and ten policemen on duty. Their task was almost impossible and although many looters were caught and arrested, most escaped detection.

Somebody set fire to kerosene cases close to the water's edge and within a short time a mass of flame distracted the law long enough for many people to escape with large quantities of wrecked goods. The flames were not extinguished for about three hours but the police had anticipated trouble and mounted officers stopped and searched almost every vehicle leaving Torquay.

In due course a horse lorry arrived at the Geelong Police Court laden with bags and boxes of tobacco, buggy shafts, sides of leather and many other articles. As the cases against the defendants proceeded the smuggled goods were transferred to the court room which soon resembled a bonded store. Penalties inflicted ranged from £25, the minimum fine under the Customs Act, and £100, the maximum allowed. Other prosecutions followed later and fines eventually exceeded £400.

People still carted goods away under cover of darkness and when chased by the police were often forced to relieve the vehicles of their load in their attempts to escape. The roads were littered with a mixture of tobacco, rolls of patent leather, axe and whip handles, household ornaments, pram wheels, clothing, kerosene and timber.

The underwriters set to work stacking salvaged goods along the beach but a high tide soon washed most of it back into the sea again, so they had a second try.

As the days passed a few still tried to smuggle goods into Geelong. One man wrapped himself in a roll of patent leather, dressed in an overcoat several sizes larger than his normal fitting, and was staggering along the road when detained by police. Another, who blatantly made three trips to the wreck on a pair horse wagon and left each time loaded with goods, finally had both goods and wagon confiscated. Twenty-nine boxes of tobacco were found buried in a trench lined with galvanised iron in the middle of a paddock sown down with barley while another visitor to the wreck who buried a couple of boxes of tobacco in his garden in Geelong and left it to mellow, found it so strong he used it as a sheep dip.

When the SCAMMELL left New York this was the cargo she carried, valued at more than £60,000:

1,500 cases of general merchandise.
400 cases of hardware.
36 packages of leather.
22 cases of clocks.
200 cases of oysters.
80 barrels of lubricating oil.
325 cases of benzine.
567 cases of tinned food.
124 bales of printing paper.
25 cases of organs.
17,625 cases of kerosene.
60 cases of medicines.
232 cases of tobacco.
6,661 tins of kerosene.

On May 13, a Geelong man, Mr W. Wallis, bought the wreck and three of her boats for £85, and three days later, at an auction held on the beach before about 800 people, Robinson, Burns and Sparrow of Geelong offered the following:

20 tons of tobacco.
1,495 yellow pine boards.
118 walnut boards.
130 rolls of paper.
35 drums of gasoline.
31 casks of resin.
49 cases of skewers.
45 cases of lubricating oil.
17 cases of axe handles (each case containing six dozen handles).
174 single shafts.
4 cases of machinery.
4 cases of tissue paper.
17 cases of shoemakers' pegs.
1 cask of window rollers.
95 Morocco hides.
Buggy wheels.
Axe handles.
2 casks of canary seed.
1 washing machine.
Shoe polish.
Large case of machinery.
5 kegs of sausage skins.
2 wringers.
8 dozen shovels.

Milling separator.
Case of oak picture frames.
Bundle of picture sticks.
Flour packing machine.
Large quantity of sundries.

The sale commenced with an offer of £5 for the 6,661 tins of kerosene and this finally reached £275. The tobacco was next. First offer for about four tons was £10, but when the buyer was told that he could also have all that was hidden on the beach he added another £10 to his bid. The tobacco eventually brought £390 but the duty brought its cost to £2,400. When the yellow pine and walnut boards came up most could not be located. The auctioneers assured the buyers that it was "either ashore or afloat" and it eventually realised £325. The leather brought £45, printing paper £32-10-0, cases of oil £65, resin £14 and miscellaneous cargo £170. All told the auction raised £1,314-10-0.

A collector of marine curiosities and wreck trophies purchased the ship's figurehead lying near Bream Creek, but when he went with a wagon to carry it away found it had been stolen.

The deck house, practically intact, was purchased by Mr W. Pride for £40 and moved with the aid of horses to its present site in Pride Street, Torquay.

A few days after the sale a number of Assyrian divers visited the wreck and demonstrated their ability to dive and recover cargo without the use of conventional diving gear.

On behalf of the syndicate which purchased some of the cargo, an auction was held at Geelong before buyers mainly from the Western District. Competition was very keen and more than £600 was taken.

At the Court of Marine Inquiry in Melbourne, Captain Chapman stated that he had no intention of entering the Heads without a pilot, but he had confused the lights of coffee houses nearby for beacons. He also considered that Split Point should be lit.

Despite supporting statements from Pilots Dennis and Mitchell the Court found that Captain Chapman had not employed sufficient care in the navigation of his ship, suspending his certificate for 12 months and ordering him to pay towards the court costs.

However, by the time the decision was reached Captain Chapman had left the State and was beyond the power of the court.

2 – Barques and Barquentines

Vessels having three or more masts, square rigged on all but the aftermast, which is fore and aft rigged. Gained in popularity when the inroads of steam forced a reduction in sailing ship crews in an attempt to compete profitably. Many ships cut down to barque rig actually gained in sailing qualities. Barquentines had three masts but carried square rigging on the foremast only, with staysails between the fore and main masts.

ISABELLA – 1837

Wooden vessel of 225 tons, built in 1826.

She left George Town, Tasmania for St. Vincent's Gulf in charge of Captain John Hart on March 29th, 1837, with twenty five people including two women and two children.

On the morning of the 31st Cape Otway was sighted and later that day land was seen from the masthead and thought to be Cape Nelson. Subsequent events showed it was probably Julia Percy Island for at about 10.15 that night she struck a perpendicular cliff without warning, smashing her bows to pieces. Within five minutes the water was over the cabin deck.

The stern and quarter boats were launched but the seas swamped them immediately. Fortunately the long boat held up enabling the crew and passengers to escape. The following morning they reached Portland Bay and were warmly received by Mr and Mrs S.G. Henty.

CHILDREN – 1839

Built at Liverpool in 1825. 224 tons burden.

Early in 1838 the CHILDREN was purchased by J. Henty and Company for use in the coastal trade and under Captain Browne completed a financially successful return voyage to London, arriving back in Launceston, Tasmania, late in November.

On the 11th January, 1839, she sailed for Adelaide with 24 passengers including 9 children, 14 crew, a mixed cargo, 1500 sheep, 8 bullocks, 7 horses and a number of farming implements, the property of Mr Bryan, one of the passengers who intended to take up land in South Australia.

Soon after sailing, hurricane force westerlies battered her, but the Victorian coast was sighted east of Portland. Visibility was poor and the barque stood off and on land for two days while Captain Browne remained undecided whether to sail for Portland and shelter until the gales abated. He had not been to bed for five days and his Chief Officer was confined to his bunk with sea sickness.

On the night of January 15 the Second Mate took charge and Captain Browne retired to his cabin for a few hours rest. The vessel was then under close reefed topsails and a fore try sail, moving north-north-west at about three knots.

At 11 o'clock that night the cry of "Breakers close ahead" brought all on deck, the helm was put up, but within a minute she struck a reef close to a small inlet in the sheer cliffs, later to be known as Childers Cove.

Within 20 minutes huge seas had taken her three masts, topside, port side, and breaking her back, leaving the stern to slip back into deep water. As the ship disintegrated those still alive were forced to the forecastle, only to be washed off one by one. Within two hours the wreck had disappeared.

Dawn revealed 22 half-naked survivors huddled on the rocks between the cliffs surrounded by the bodies of their unfortunate companions, stock and wreckage. Those drowned were the Captain, Second Mate, three sailors, two men passengers, a lady passenger and four of her children, also four other children. All the sheep, and most of the horses and cattle were also lost.

Mr Bryan was lucky to escape. Shortly before the barque broke up the anchor fell on his foot, pinning it to the deck and tearing the first joints off three toes. Later, on shore, a fourth toe was amputated with a knife.

Leaving most of the survivors camped on the beach near the wreck, a small party led by First Mate Gaye set out to obtain help. Being uncertain of their position, they believed Port Fairy lay to the east but the sight of wild desolate country as far as the eye could see brought the realisation of their approximate position, so after resting they set out to the west. Aborigines were often seen at a distance but they did not approach, and so after several days help was obtained from Captain Campbell's farm near Port Fairy. Word was sent to Portland and soon after carts arrived to carry the survivors to the settlement where they received medical attention from a surgeon who had recently arrived from Kangaroo Island on the SOCRATES. Later, both the SOCRATES and SALLY ANN returned the survivors to Launceston.

Late in 1951, shifting sands exposed skeletons at Childers Cove which were generally accepted as relics of the disaster and in recent years skin divers have located portion of the wreck. In 1963 Warrnambool skin divers recovered a cannon four feet six inches in length with a bore of three and a half inches, also believed to have come from the wreck.

MARY ANN (MARY) – 1840

Built at Bristol in 1821. 276 tons.

The barque MARY ANN was reported by the Port Phillip Patriot as having been wrecked at Port Fairy in September when a severe storm drove her ashore. She carried a full cargo of whale oil.

SOCRATES – 1843

Built 1821. 152 tons. Registered at Launceston.

After arriving at Port Fairy from Portland with a full cargo on August 28th, the barque SOCRATES put out two anchors in about three fathoms and was preparing to unload some cargo when a heavy southerly gale sprang up.

For two days heavy squalls and mountainous seas battered the vessel until both anchors parted on August 30 and she drifted ashore to lie on her beam ends, bilged and filled with water.

When the storm abated her master, Captain Grant, still retained high hopes that she could be refloated until a board of masters examined her and declared her a total loss. She was offered for auction a few days later, the wreck bringing £45 and the cargo £15.

This is the cargo she carried:

60 tons oil casks.	10 tons hay.
408 bags flour.	10 tons coal.
342 bags bran.	10 casks bottled beer.
20 bags wheat.	1 dressing machine.
1½ tons potatoes.	1 smutting machine.
40 bags biscuits.	20 bags sugar.
20 tons mixed timber.	4 chests tea.
2000 palings.	7000 feet cedar.

LYDIA – 1847

Built 1825. 277 tons. Registered at Liverpool.

The LYDIA arrived at Port Fairy and anchored in only three fathoms although drawing 13 feet, her master, Captain Petrie, being misled by one of the crew who had visited the port several times, claiming that the water was much deeper.

On the night of February 2nd the sea rose suddenly and in the swell the LYDIA struck several times, driving up her sternpost and causing serious damage along her keel. Taking water rapidly, she was run ashore and eventually abandoned although most of her cargo was recovered.

Some time later the hull was sold to Captain Griffiths, who repaired and refloated her, only to lose her when she leaked so badly she was again run ashore and eventually dismantled.

PRINCESS ROYAL – 1849

426 tons.

The PRINCESS ROYAL, Captain Sinclair, inward bound from Hong Kong with a cargo of silk, tea, sugar and wine, struck the Lonsdale Reef at 3 a.m. on the morning of February 24th, and became a total wreck. The crew barely had time to launch the long boat and cutter before she went to pieces.

In his report to Lloyd's agents, Captain Sinclair stated that the light on the inner head near Queenscliff had led him into danger. He was using an old chart of the Heads and the barque had run ashore before he realised his exact position.

The sea threw her across the reef and on the third surge she bumped so hard she broke in two, scattering her cargo over a wide area. Very little was recovered.

Valued at about £5,000, the remains were sold for a mere £20.

MARIE - 1851

450 tons.

The German barque MARIE, Captain Rathje, from Antwerp to Adelaide, then Sydney, with 25 passengers and crew, was wrecked near Cape Bridgewater early in September. There were no survivors.

She arrived in Port Adelaide on August 20th, then left for Sydney on September 12th with some cargo and passengers, including the Belgian Consul and his staff.

Almost a month passed before reports circulated through the district and back to the main ports that a vessel had been lost on a wild section of coastline about 12 miles west of Portland.

A party from the Mount Gambier district searched the coast and recovered a large quantity of cargo and wreckage which lay scattered over more than 30 miles. Six badly mutilated bodies were subsequently washed ashore, followed by three more a few days later, while large sections of the vessel were washed up weeks later at Cape Otway and Apollo Bay.

Settlers near the scene of the wreck stated that they had seen a barque beat out of Bridgewater Bay during a heavy gale in September and that night gunfire was heard out to sea.

MEROPE - 1853

The barque MEROPE, 311 tons left Portland on February 16th for Swan River with 125 passengers and a mixed cargo but adverse winds forced her well off course and she went ashore near the mouth of the Fitzroy River. No lives were lost but the vessel bacame a total wreck.

ARCHER - 1853

A vessel of 237 tons, built in 1830.

The barque ARCHER, loading wheat in Lady Bay, parted her chains in a light south-easterly on November 8th, and drifted ashore, much to the astonishment of local residents.

She was refloated, but shortly after drifted ashore a second time about 100 yards east of the jetty and became a total wreck although her cargo of 1037 bags of wheat was unloaded, while her masts and rigging were also salvaged.

Before she was dismantled it was suggested that the hull could be converted into a beach refreshment house with the deck altered for promenading and dancing, but this was rejected.

The local newspaper's outspoken comments on the loss of the vessel almost involved the editor in a libel suit. Richard Osburne in the "Examiner" was outspoken concerning the barque's anchor chains, claiming they were not much thicker than bullock chains. He also hinted that she was wrecked to collect insurance.

INELLAN - 1854

Vessel of 288 tons, built in 1852.

Early on the morning of February 17th, one of the worst storms in the history of Port Fairy destroyed two vessels and caused considerable damage.

The barque INELLAN, moored with two anchors and special riding tackle, parted both her anchors and drove ashore where she soon became a total wreck. Most of her cargo was also lost.

DUNDEE – 1854

Vessel of 346 tons, built in 1840.

A short distance away, the same gale destroyed the barque DUNDEE, which was loaded with about 900 bales of wool for London.

She was riding at one of the Government moorings but the ropes parted, tearing out her windlass, and she began to drag towards the beach. In drifting she fouled the ship BENJAMIN ELKIN, also for London with wool, but broke clear and went to pieces on the beach.

NESTOR – 1854

Built 1840. 458 tons.

The wreck of the NESTOR at Portland on October 27th caused a mild sensation when three auger holes were found in her hull. The Captain, Second Mate and Carpenter were committed for trial on the charge of deliberately scuttling the vessel, but were found not guilty.

The NESTOR had arrived at Portland ten days previously with 166 immigrants and a cargo of railway iron for Madras. She was lying at anchor preparing for her outward voyage when the leak was discovered. Soundings were taken and ten inches of water were found in the hold. Within an hour the depth of water had increased to six feet, and when a later sounding showed seven feet the master, Captain Brown, slipped both chains and allowed the vessel to drift ashore, capsizing a lighter which happened to be in its way. The pumps were kept going night and day for nearly a fortnight while the vessel was lying on the beach but the water was only reduced to four or five feet, and the ship eventually went to pieces; but not before some divers went down and discovered three large auger holes in the hull under the captain's cabin.

Captain Brown appeared most surprised, but the authorities quickly laid charges and had the men arrested before they could disappear. Meanwhile, most of the crew gradually drifted away and were presumed to have headed for the goldfields.

AUSTRALASIA – 1855

485 tons, built in 1847.

On Monday, March 19th, a strong south-easterly gale rolled a heavy sea into Portland Bay, causing shipping anchored there to pitch and roll heavily.

By evening, two barques, the CONSTANT and AUSTRALASIA, had each parted a cable, but had soon replaced them with sheet anchors and sent out signals of distress.

Near midnight, the AUSTRALASIA dragged her remaining anchors into the breakers and lay across a ledge of rocks, listing to seaward and broken amidships. Within a few hours she had broken up, scattering about 800 bales of wool into the sea.

About 500 bales were eventually recovered and purchased along with the wreck by Stephen and Francis Henty who, after fellmongering and rebaling, shipped it to London, where it realised a profit of more than £9,000.

CONSTANT - 1855

525 tons, built in 1843.

The gale which blew the AUSTRALASIA ashore also destroyed the CONSTANT.

Near midnight the CONSTANT, in ballast only, parted her starboard and port anchors before driving on to the beach where she remained upright with good prospects of being refloated. However, a survey made a few days later recommended that she be sold. Her buyers employed workmen to break her up before she went to pieces.

The Portland Harbour Master, Captain Fawthrop, examined the anchorage, then reported that the anchors of both vessels had held and their loss was caused by defective anchor chains.

GRANGE - 1858

Built at Troon, Scotland, in 1840, and owned by T. Shaw, who operated her regularly between the Clyde and Penang. 301 tons.

The Henty Reef, extending for about two miles from the shore at Marengo, south of Apollo Bay, is cut in several places by deep channels, and at its extremities rises to within 18 feet of the surface causing huge rollers to break unexpectedly during tide changes or bad weather. Local fishermen give it a wide berth.

The barque GRANGE, commanded by Captain Alexander, was towed from her anchorage at Hobson's Bay on Wednesday, March 24th, 1858, by the tug LIONESS, on a voyage to Singapore via Guam.

Her trip to the heads was uneventful and she passed Point Lonsdale at 5.30 p.m. heading south-west into a slight swell. At 10 p.m. light rain commenced falling and continued throughout the night, bringing a considerable reduction in visibility. Full sail was set in the light breeze and the log recorded a speed of about seven knots.

Just before dawn the Mate reported a light W.N.W. and summoned the Captain but it was not seen again. Shortly after 5 a.m. breakers were heard, but no land was visible. Captain Alexander realising he was off course consulted his chart but believed the vessel was still well south of Cape Otway.

A few minutes later they were in breakers. The helm was put hard down in an attempt to pull the vessel around, but as the yards could not be trimmed, she continued on and struck an outcrop of the Henty Reef a glancing blow, slowly coming up into the wind before falling away. The strong current surging around the reef carried the helpless vessel closer to shore as waves washed her from stem to stern.

31

The Captain attempted to back the GRANGE through a gap in the reef, but after driving astern for considerable distance she struck aft on a rock and remained fast. Soundings showed water in the holds but she did not appear in any immediate danger, being partly protected by the reef.

The crew launched a boat, rowed out 400 yards to the beach and were able to ascertain their position from the small group of settlers who had hurried to the scene.

Later in the day heavy seas began pounding the vessel and the Captain, realising that his ship was doomed, unbent the sails and landed them on the beach, together with the stores and all moveable gear.

News of the wreck reached Melbourne late on March 25th when Commander Purvis of the steamship MOEGAERA reported GRANGE on shore bilged and with her rudder gone.

Heavy seas battered the vessel for a week, carrying away portion of the decking and masts and precipitating much wreckage on the beach. A local syndicate purchased the wreck and succeeded in removing most fittings of value before it broke up about a month later. The remains lay on a reef and beach for about 20 years, exposed at low tide, but the sea and sand have now completely removed all traces.

TAMORA - 1860

A vessel of 419 tons, built at Dundee in 1853.

Friday, November 16th, dawned bright and clear with a moderate easterly wind, but by mid-afternoon it had increased to a gale, causing concern for vessels anchored in Portland Bay.

At 5 p.m., with the surf running very high, the barque TAMORA, lightly loaded and drawing only 13 feet, fired cannon to attract attention then signalled she had bumped heavily in about four fathoms, and was taking water.

Although the pumps were manned, the water gained steadily and rose to six feet in the hold in less than half an hour. At 11 p.m., with the water still rising, the cables were slipped and the vessel ran ashore. Immediately she grounded she fell on her side and in order to prevent her breaking up, the fore and main masts were cut away. However, by 2 a.m. next morning she had become a total wreck.

At daylight the harbour crew fastened a line and the fourteen hands reached safety.

Some of the cargo, which drifted ashore practically undamaged was stored in the Customs House yard until sold by auction, along with the wreck, for £1800.

JANE - 1863

208 tons.

Although the crew of the barque JANE, bound from Adelaide to Otago, and wrecked near Cape Bridgewater on June 6th, reached safety, one of the rescuers, C. Hedditch of Bridgewater, was washed off the rocks and drowned.

Squally weather and strong inshore currents forced the vessel ashore and word was immediately sent overland to Portland. Captain Fawthrop sent the lifeboat around to the wreck, then proceeded to the scene with the rocket crew and their gear.

The vessel was lying on a ledge of rocks with her masts gone and surf crashing over her. Three rockets were fired without success, but eventually a cask with line attached was floated ashore, then a heavy hawser was secured.

Eight members of the crew were able to struggle ashore along this line, but as darkness fell, the Captain decided to remain on board overnight.

Fawthrop signalled the lifeboat to return to Portland and soon after dawn, the Captain reached the shore safely.

MARIE GABRIELLE – 1869

The three-masted barque of 258 tons, built at Nantes, France, in 1864.

During the nineteenth century, the Chinese port of Foochow, developed as an export centre for tea, and ships from all over the world sailed there to load from the thousands of sampans gathered on the river.

The French barque, MARIE GABRIELLE, which had visited Melbourne on several occasions, left Foochow on September 5th, 1869, with a cargo of 302,400 lbs. of tea for Melbourne merchants and was favoured by fine weather and steady winds until she reached the Victorian coast.

At 7 p.m. on November 24th, soon after passing Cape Bridgewater, a strong south-westerly gale forced her to shorten sail, after which she became difficult to hold on course, and despite the desperate efforts of Captain Blanchard and his crew, she was driven ashore at Wreck Beach near Moonlight Head, at 1 a.m. on the following morning.

Fortunately, the barque was driven through a narrow channel in the reef to a sandy basin, and at dawn all landed safely by boat. Unfortunately, it was swamped and smashed on the beach before the men clambered out, littering the beach with personal belongings, although Captain Blanchard saved the ship's papers and log book.

After a short rest, the crew decided to separate. Captain Blanchard, the Mate and three of the crew arrived at Cape Otway three days later, in great distress, having been without food for four days. Despite language difficulties, Captain Blanchard conveyed full particulars to the lightkeeper, who telegraphed the information to Melbourne. During the journey from the wreck, they had used their clothes as ropes to lower each other down the cliffs.

The Second Mate and five men reached Chappel and Laurie's station on the Aire River on the same day. Another crew member rested at Moonlight Head, while four Maoris remained at the wreck subsisting on limpets and grass roots.

Captain Blanchard believed that most of the cargo could be salvaged, so at the request of the Marine Insurance Companies, the Harbour Master, Captain Helpman, with Sergeant Archibald, left Warrnambool and travelled fifty-three miles overland to the wreck, being joined on the way by Dr. Curdie, Hugh Gibson and a group of shearers who were shearing at Glenample Station.

Local residents informed them that the barque had spent the afternoon prior to the wreck tacking close in shore, and soon after she struck residents at Glenample heard shots.

The vessel was found lying close up under the cliff with her bow pointing to the shore. The hull had broken in two horizontally from stem to stern, the keel having disappeared, and the bow lying between two large rocks. Portion of the poop, forecastle, and stumps of the masts were visible from the shore. The figurehead was lying on the beach and hundreds of chests of tea were floating in the surf. The only livestock on board were a pig, a captive albatross, and a cat. Discovering a tin of preserved meat the sergeant opened it and gave the contents to the starving animals, which had not eaten for nearly a week.

Curdie and Gibson, anticipating looting as strangers began arriving on the scene, sent a messenger to the Insurance Company representative at Warrnambool offering £20 for the wreck and cargo. The company immediately sent an auctioneer and the cargo was knocked down to Gibson for £1-10-0. When the wreck was auctioned there were no bids, so the ship and cargo were passed to Curdie and Gibson for £20, the original offer.

The men set to work with a team of bullocks and soon collected everything they considered of value. The tier of tea chests about three feet deep along the base of the cliffs at Wreck Beach, damaged by salt water, was left. The goods were divided into three lots, one saleable, such as new ropes and sails; and lots were drawn for the other two lots. Then, the saleable lot was sent to Geelong where it brought £70.

The firm of McGhee & Co. of Melbourne wrote to Curdie and Gibson advising that they had also bought the wreck, but when they received the reply that they could have it if they paid the salvage, nothing more was heard.

OLIVIA DAVIS – 1855

Built 1874. 523 tons. Length, 135.1 feet; beam, 31.2 feet; depth, 17 feet.

Caught by a south-easterly, the barque OLIVIA DAVIS, commanded by Captain Sipple, was driven ashore near the Warrnambool lighthouse where she became a total wreck.

She and the barque PROSPECTOR, were loading in Lady Bay on May 4th, when the gale blew up without warning, endangering both vessels. During the night the OLIVIA DAVIS broke from her anchors and drifted towards shore, but by next day, with the weather moderating, she remained to complete her loading.

However, during the next night, the wind rose again bringing huge seas and heavy squalls which battered the vessel, tearing away anchors and leaving her holding only by her starboard tackle.

Those on shore, realising her danger, sent out two lifeboats, and after many anxious moments, Captain Sipple, his wife and members of the crew were taken off, leaving the barque pitching and rolling in an alarming fashion just beyond the line of breakers.

Eventually, the OLIVIA DAVIS was driven on to the beach, but hopes of refloating her were dashed when a close examination revealed considerable damage, and she was eventually sold by auction.

The Steam Navigation Board exonerated Captain Sipple of all blame for her loss, congratulating him and the crew on their attention to duty.

GEORGE ROPER – 1883

Built 1882. 2033 tons. Length 301.7 feet; beam 39 feet; depth 23.6 feet.

The four-masted barque GEORGE ROPER, inward bound to Melbourne on her maiden voyage with a general cargo, including £20,000 worth of rails for the Victorian Government, ran into fog while entering the Heads in tow of the paddle steamer WILLIAMS, on July 4th.

The tug struck the Point Lonsdale Reef and was so seriously damaged that she was forced to release the tow line and make for Queenscliff, leaving the barque helpless in the fog, with the result that she herself ran on to the reef. The Queenscliff lifeboat was immediately called to her assistance, and S.S. DAWN, from Portland, also stood by.

Tugs were sent from Melbourne to tow the vessel off, but they were unsuccessful, and all hope of saving the ship was abandoned. Several lighters were towed to the scene, but by this time a big crowd had gathered on the beach, many of them camping the night in Buckley's Cave, with a view to collecting anything that floated ashore. However, local police and the lighthouse keeper remained on watch throughout the night.

The ship bumped heavily on the reef and began taking water as the steamers, ALBATROSS, BLACK BOY, and CLEOPATRA, assisted by the schooner AGNES, removed portion of the cargo including a quantity of dynamite. Three days after the wreck, the ship, which cost £70,000, and the cargo, valued at £50,000, were sold by auction to Mr Alfred Shaw, on behalf of a Melbourne syndicate for £3,600.

Mr Shaw visited the wreck and found that hundreds of tons of drapery and other goods were quite dry, while the main cabin was above water. The BLACK BOY was employed to unload this cargo, but on July 8th, she lurched heavily whilst lying alongside the wreck, carrying away her funnel. However, as it was secured by hinges it merely fell to the deck, taking the mast with it. Temporary repairs were effected, and as she started away with a full load of cargo, a mooring line fouled her propeller throwing her against the ship. She swung with the tide and rapidly drifted into the breakers, where she bumped heavily. The Queenscliff lifeboat was called, but the vessel was shipping heavy seas, necessitating the jettisoning of a quantity of her cargo. A rocket was fired from the lighthouse but this fell short, and it was left to rescue the twelve men aboard.

After landing the BLACK BOY's crew, the lifeboat proceeded to the GEORGE ROPER and took off all men working on her. S.S. PHAROS, using a boat, attempted to remove the BLACK BOY's cargo but it was found impossible to get close in, owing to the rough seas.

The BLACK BOY was sold to the GEORGE ROPER syndicate for £200, but, unfortunately for them, she was lifted clean off the rocks by a heavy sea and went down stern first into deep water. As soon as she sank, her decks burst open, and the cargo floated to the surface to be picked up by the steamers, FLEETWING and PHAROS.

The steamer SPRAY, which replaced the BLACK BOY, narrowly escaped a similar fate when leaving the GEORGE ROPER with a cargo. A rope fouled her propeller, but fortunately the diver from the wreck was able to clear it before she drifted on to the reef.

Most of the cargo was salvaged before the GEORGE ROPER went to pieces during a gale on August 26th.

Following an inquiry the Pilot Board found the pilot guilty of negligence in approaching the entrance and suspended his certificate for two years.

SOUTH MILTON – 1886

Built at Sunderland in 1877. 598 tons. Length, 159 feet; beam, 30.7 feet; depth, 17.9 feet.

The wooden barque SOUTH MILTON, Captain Trinnick, left Mauritius with a crew of 16 and a cargo of sugar on March 7th, but struck the Charlemont Reef near Barwon Heads at 4 a.m. on April 10th, about a mile southwest from the Bluff.

The master had been proceeding carefully up the coast taking soundings and when the lead gave 17 fathoms, he believed the ship safe, although the land seemed very close. The lookout, the master's nephew, did not report broken water marking the reef and the ship struck twice in the heavy seas forcing the crew into the rigging.

One of the apprentices who was in his bunk suffering from Mauritius fever was carried to the highest position for safety.

The seas forced the barque over the reef into calmer water, enabling the crew to launch the boats and escape with a few bundles of clothes.

Soon after they left, compressed air trapped below the vessel blew the poop and portion of the deck high into the air as the vessel broke up and was washed into 9 fathoms of water.

The pilot schooner RIP picked up the survivors and took them to Queenscliff, and from there they were towed to the Quarantine Station for inspection by the Health Officer.

The Steam Navigation Board held an inquiry on April 15th and found that the barque was wrecked in consequence of the default of the master, Captain H. Trinnick, by not using reasonable care and precaution in navigating his vessel when approaching Port Phillip Heads, by not taking bearings of the Cape Schanck light and verifying those bearings by soundings, and, when he became doubtful of his position, in not putting his vessel's head to the southward.

His certificate was suspended for three months.

The remains of the ship and her boats were sold at auction on the beach for £12, while the cargo brought a mere 11/-.

GLANEUSE – 1886

Built 1870. 481 tons. Length, 152.6 feet; beam, 26.6 feet; depth, 17 feet.

The French barque GLANEUSE left Charente on May 28th, with a capacity cargo of wine, brandy and sardines for Melbourne, Launceston, Hobart, Sydney and Dunedin.

The vessel arrived off Port Phillip Heads at dusk on October 1st, but after failing to pick up a pilot, beat about off Torquay for several hours before coasting back towards the Heads. However, instead of keeping out to sea in view of the lighthouse, she hugged the shore and ran into a channel between the mainland and a reef near Point Lonsdale.

At about 1 a.m. on October 2nd, Captain Gorse, finding that the current was driving the vessel on to the land, let go the starboard anchor, but by this time the barque was bumping heavily on the rocks.

No signals of distress were fired, and the lighthouse keeper did not realise the vessel was ashore until 4 a.m., but he quickly alerted the Queenscliff lifeboat and the tug, AVON.

Mr Dickson, the Custom's Coastwaiter at Queenscliff, took the rocket apparatus from Point Lonsdale and fired a line aboard the vessel between the main and mizzen masts, to bring the crew ashore.

At low tide on the following day, a couple of spars were fastened from the vessel's stern to the beach and about 150 cases of brandy were skidded down to the stevedores who were standing up to the waists in water. Customs Officers Ford and McGowan of Melbourne, and Bennie, Thomas and Green of Geelong, took charge of the cargo, but several disturbances occurred among the crew, who had pillaged portion of the cargo before the officers arrived. A wire rope was afterwards run from the high sand hills to the barque and fastened to the mizzen mast, and by this means all the cargo was eventually landed.

GANGE – 1887

Built 1885. 1,071 tons. Length, 152 feet; beam, 30.1 feet; depth, 16.8 feet.

This Austrian barque inward bound for Melbourne with twenty passengers and crew, including the wife and daughter of the master, Captain Ivaneich, went ashore on the Point Lonsdale Reef on the night of July 23rd.

The lifeboat left Queenscliff, but the sea was very choppy, preventing the rescue of the crew until after daylight.

The loss of the GLANEUSE and GANGE in less than twelve months brought a storm of criticism against the Pilot Service and a subsequent streamlining of the service.

EDINBURGH CASTLE – 1888

Built 1863. 627 tons. Length, 176.3 feet; beam, 29.5 feet; depth, 18.7 feet.

The barque EDINBURGH CASTLE, out from London with 4,900 casks of cement for the Warrnambool breakwater, missed stays when wearing into Lady Bay on January 15th, and was carried by a gust of wind towards shore.

Fearing damage if the anchors were lowered in shallow water, Captain Darling ordered a kedge dropped to steady her, but when this cable parted under the strain, the vessel bumped heavily before settling in the sand.

The relieving Harbour Master and Pilot, Captain Carless, who had boarded the barque as she entered the bay, then obtained an anchor which was dropped at the stern to hold her while the unloading of the cement into lighters commenced. This was found to be too slow, so early next morning casks were jettisoned as quickly as possible.

The JULIA PERCY, sent from Portland, tried vainly for several hours to tow her clear, but when the hawser parted the attempt was abandoned. The captain and most of the crew of seventeen then went ashore, leaving the Mate, a seaman and a lighterman on board.

Meanwhile, word of the barque's plight was telegraphed to Melbourne and her agents decided to put her up for auction on the Saturday.

On the Friday evening, rough seas commenced to batter the barque but the rocket crew were quickly summoned to carry their gear two miles around the beach. They fastened a line at their third attempt and the three men were landed safely. By morning the EDINBURGH CASTLE was lying broadside on to the beach and breaking up fast.

Word was sent to Melbourne, but in the meantime she had been sold to H. Thompson for £520. Next day her back broke, leaving only the bow and stern visible, and scattering wreckage and cargo for miles along the beach. Very little was saved.

The Pilot Board found that the acting pilot, Captain Carless, had made an error of judgment, but apart from a censure, no further action was taken.

HOLYHEAD – 1890

Built 1889. 2,260 tons. Length, 294 feet; beam, 42 feet; depth, 24.5 feet.

On Wednesday afternoon, February 12th, a message was received at Geelong from Barwon Heads to the effect that a large four-masted barque with all sails set had been seen coming round the Bluff as if making for the mouth of the Barwon, when suddenly the sound of a gun was heard, then the ship went about and headed for Cape Schanck. She was so close in that, had the tide been low, she must inevitably have run on to the rocks.

The ship proved to be the HOLYHEAD, commanded by Captain Williams, on her maiden voyage, 74 days out from Liverpool, having been completed only a month before she sailed. She had signalled for a pilot for three hours, and, finding her signals could not be seen in the misty weather, the captain decided to run in towards the land. The vessel was next seen off Point Lonsdale by the assistant lighthouse keeper, and was then attempting to tack. The pilot schooner, RIP, attempted to warn her, but she was too far to leeward to be reached as she drifted rapidly towards the reef.

Every effort was made to bring the ship round, but in mid-afternoon she struck the reef close to where the GEORGE ROPER had been lost. Water commenced to flow in rapidly, and, within a few minutes, seven feet were registered in the hold as the wind increased to a gale, driving the seas over her.

The lifeboat from Queenscliff ran alongside after a rough trip through the Rip, taking off all hands except the Chief Officer and Carpenter, who were left on board, as the ship showed no signs of breaking up. The steamer ALBATROSS arrived later at the wreck, but could not communicate due to the heavy sea running, but during a temporary lull, the Geelong Customs Officer, Mr P. Holden, was able to board her.

A quantity of soft goods consigned to various Melbourne warehouses, was placed on board the tug, together with the crew's effects, but, after a few hours the wind and sea commenced to freshen again, and the operations had to be discontinued. The cargo recovered, valued at about £1,500, was placed in the Customs shed at Queenscliff.

On the day after the wreck the ketch LU LU arrived at Queenscliff in tow of the tug PILOT, but an attempt to reach the wreck was unsuccessful, owing to the freshening wind and an incoming tide. In the evening the ALBATROSS returned from Melbourne with a gang of men and several mooring buoys, and proceeded to the wreck with the intention of laying moorings for the lighters, but had to return to Queenscliff on account of the heavy seas.

After two days, the Chief Officer and Carpenter, who had remained on board were so frightened at night by the force of the seas on the stranded ship, that they signalled for assistance and were taken off by the lifeboat. They stated that portion of the deck aft was gradually being forced upwards.

Thousands of sightseers visited the cliffs above the wreck over several weekends, and the Sunday Bay excursion steamers were packed with passengers from Melbourne and Geelong.

Five days after the wreck the sails were stripped from the masts, and a tug took a full load of miscellaneous goods and cabin fittings to Melbourne, leaving on board 32 stevedores, a diver, assistant, and two Customs officers.

As time went on and the removal of cargo lightened the ship, she began to bump heavily on the reef and after an unsuccessful attempt to tow the vessel off on March 11th, salvage operations were discontinued, and the wreck was sold to a syndicate.

The ship's cargo included 1,000 tons of slates and a similar quantity of iron rails, bars and rods. The slates were not considered worth salvaging, but, being stowed on top of the iron, had to be removed, and they were dumped in the sea beside the wreck. The iron rods, in various lengths, and some less than half an inch in diameter, were hauled up in bundles from the hold to a sufficient height to enable them to be landed into a lighter moored a few feet from the side of the wreck. It was while one of these bundles was suspended in midair, preparatory to being swung into the lighter, that the first serious accident occurred. One of the stevedores was looking up at the sling with his mouth open, when an iron rod fell out end first and entered his mouth, coming out under his chin.

During the next three months a large quantity of cargo was recovered, but most of the profit was lost in attempts to get the ship off. The pumping plant alone cost £3000.

In the middle of July a spell of heavy weather put an end to their hopes of refloating the vessel, and the engines and gear were landed at Queenscliff. The ship's stern had been stove in by the constant battering of the seas, and the hull was badly strained.

The wreck was purchased for dismantling and the mizzenmast and a number of spars had been taken down ready for removal when a violent storm washed them over the side, carrying the whole of the midship bulwarks on the port side. The mainmast fell with a crash, clearing away the starboard bulwarks and plates of the hull, and causing the ship to open up and settle down with a strong list to port.

The jiggermast was still standing erect, but only the fore part of the vessel and the foremast were above water. During the next two weeks the beach between Point Lonsdale and Queenscliff was strewn with deck planking, fittings, bulkheads, hatches, and other debris. A fortnight later, the foremast fell over the side and completed the destruction of the ship, a little over six months after she struck.

A Court of Marine Inquiry found that the captain did not make proper efforts to ascertain the position of the ship after sighting Cape Otway and approaching Port Phillip Heads. That he was not justified in not using the lead. That he steered a dangerous course and carried too much sail. That he did not make sufficient efforts to obtain a pilot. That he was not on deck when he ought to have been, and that the ship was not navigated with proper and seamanlike care. That his careless navigation amounted to gross misconduct.

The Court also found against the Mate.

The master's certificate was suspended for two years, and the mate's for eighteen months, and they were ordered to pay £20 and £10 towards the expenses of the inquiry.

W.B. GODFREY – 1891

Built at Greenock, Scotland, in 1861, and originally named MIN. Purchased in 1888 by a syndicate of Hawaiian citizens for the Pacific Islands trade, and registered in Honolulu. 651 tons. Length, 174.5 feet; beam, 29.8 feet; depth, 19.3 feet.

In January 1891, the vessel, commanded by Charles Davies, sailed from San Francisco with seven passengers and a cargo of timber. Also on board were the captain's wife and child.

Although the weather was favourable throughout, the voyage was not without incident. Soon after sailing, the Second Mate was confined to his bunk with rheumatism, and remained there during the fifty-six days of the voyage, the First Mate, J. Garthley, quarrelled with the captain, and insubordination among officers and men steadily increased. Full credit must go to Mrs Davies, who stood by her husband, and even took watch to enable him to rest.

On the evening of March 7th, the Captain estimated that his ship was approaching Port Phillip Heads, although due to a miscalculation caused by dense smoke from bushfires in the Otways, he was some twenty miles to the west.

At 7 o'clock on the same night, the captain was on deck looking for Cape Schanck when the lookout, a seaman named Edwards, reported land on the starboard quarter. The captain, mistaking the call "land" for "light" kept on course until his mistake was pointed out by a member of the crew. Immediately, orders were given to "wear ship" but the vessel, slow to respond, struck rocks west of Lorne where a small stream now known as the Godfrey River, enters the sea. The Chief Officer was rowed ashore and was able to ascertain that the ship was many miles west of the Heads.

More sail was set, about 10,000 feet of timber jettisoned, but the GODFREY remained fast. Next morning a search was made for a settlement, and a shelter built for the passengers and crew. The same evening, the ketch JESSIE on a voyage from Lorne to Apollo Bay sighted the wreck and towed the passengers and crew to Lorne in a ship's lifeboat.

The Government steamer, LADY LOCH, and the tug RACER, spent several hours without success trying to free the GODFREY, and eventually, heavy weather lifted the hull almost onto the beach.

Although the Captain later denied that he had seriously miscalculated his position, men employed in the erection of the Split Point Lighthouse noticed the barque close in to Airey's Inlet the day before she was lost. After standing in near shore for some time, the vessel had put about and sailed away in the direction of King Island for about 20 miles before turning back towards the coast.

On April 18th, a small dinghy carrying five men engaged in salvage operations, capsized in rough seas when attempting a landing on the wreck from the barque CHITTOOR, and the Mate, R. Pleace, and a seaman, J. McIntyre, were drowned. McIntyre's body was not recovered. Prior to his engagement as First Mate on the CHITTOOR, Pleace had served as Harbour Master at Geelong for 15 years. Mr Burns, the overseer, believed that the drownings might have been avoided if the small steamer HOPE, also used in the operations, had not been absent at Lorne at the time of the accident.

On June 18th, a second accident occurred when a heavy sea again capsized

41

a boat from the CHITTOOR. Five men were in the boat and four swam to safety. The fifth, Charles Boulter, could not swim and was drowned, his body finally washing ashore near Barwon Heads nearly a month later.

Salvage work continued until September 6th, but then, the CHITTOOR returned to Melbourne where her master, Captain Gortley, chartered the schooner CLARA to load the estimated 20,000 feet of timber still lying on the beach.

At about 7 a.m. on the morning of October 8th, yet another dinghy was capsized as a kedge anchor was being raised near the stern of the CLARA. Three men, Gobert, Godfrey and Radegoude were thrown into the sea. Godfrey, being a good swimmer, struck out for the CLARA, but the other two clung to the boat until it drifted on to the beach. Captain Gortley, the only man on the CLARA, lowered a dinghy and made towards Godfrey, but his boat also capsized. Gortley, fully clothed and wearing sea boots sank immediately, while Godfrey also disappeared in full view of the men standing helplessly on the beach beside the boat, but without oars. Both bodies were later recovered and buried on the low cliff overlooking the wreck.

Salvage operations were abandoned and the incident was forgotten until 1930, when the C.R.B. was constructing the Wye River section of the Great Ocean Road. Right in the path of the proposed road workmen found a weatherbeaten wooden peg recording vague references to the tragedy.

The C.R.B. was anxious to retain a record of early history in the area, but few could recall the wreck, although there were several conflicting stories. A permanent headstone was erected, but discrepancies crept in due, no doubt, to difficulty in reading the lettering. The new headstone read:

ERECTED BY C.R.B.
WYE RIVER CAMP, MAY 1930.
IN MEMORY OF
CAPTAIN DOBEL PALICE AND GODFREY,
DROWNED OFF SHIP W.B. GODFREY,
MARCH 1891.

The wording and its arrangement caused much confusion. Dobel is not known, Pleace is mis-spelt, and the others, Boulter and Gortley, apparently forgotten.

However, the beach at this point has a considerable amount of rusted wreckage, and the remains of the GODFREY may be seen on the rocks about twenty-five yards out to sea. Skin divers say most of the wreck lies further out in deeper water.

During very low tide it is possible to closely examine the remains and search for likely souvenirs.

The headstone was broken into two pieces by vandals in 1963, but the inscription was not damaged, being repaired by encasing in concrete. Then, in 1965, it was re-erected in a slightly different position at the head of a false grave; the bodies of the drowned seamen remain buried beneath the present road pavement, but the grave was updated in 1988.

FIJI - 1891

Built at Belfast 1875. 1,436 tons gross. Length, 229.3 feet; beam, 36.3 feet; depth, 23.1 feet.

A weatherbeaten headstone on the cliffs, 200 feet above Wreck Beach, recalls one of the most sensational and spectacular wrecks ever to occur on the Victorian coast.

The barque FIJI, commanded by Captain Vickers, inward bound from Hamburg to Melbourne with a crew of twenty and a general cargo including 200 cases of dynamite, was nearing Cape Otway early on Sunday morning, September 6th, 1891, when the Second Mate reported land about five miles off the lee bow. An attempt was made to go on to the other tack, but she missed stays. Captain Vickers then tried to wear her, but no sooner had the helm been put up and the main yard squared, than she struck rocks about 300 yards from the shore, only a short distance west from where the MARIE GABRIELLE had been lost twenty-two years earlier.

Efforts were made to lower boats, while rockets were fired and blue lights burned, but huge seas swept the ship, swamping the cabins and carrying away all the steering gear. Within a few minutes, the twenty-six members of the crew were driven to the forecastle head, bowsprit and jibboom and there they clung expecting the ship to go to pieces or be washed off into the raging surf.

At daybreak, two men volunteered to make an effort to reach the shore with a line. A Russian, Daniel Katlien, was swept away and drowned, but a Spaniard named Julius Gebauhr, reached the shore at his second attempt after cutting the line when it became entangled in kelp and began to pull him under. He was discovered soon after by a party of Warrnambool residents, who were inspecting land for selection, and taken to the Rivernook guest house, then owned by Mr John Evans. Gebauhr was astounded when told the position of the wreck, believing that Melbourne was only about ten miles to the east.

Messengers were sent to Port Campbell for the rocket crew, and Warrnambool for the lifeboat, but as the afternoon wore on with no sign of help, the ship's carpenter plunged into the sea and struck out for the shore. As his strength faded, the undertow took him out to sea, but a young settler named Arthur Wilkinson, swam out to the drowning man and attempted to help him ashore. Two or three times he almost reached the beach but, finally, with his strength failing, he swam with his charge back to the ship where both were hauled on board and laid on the forecastle head. The carpenter revived and was later rescued, but when the last man left the FIJI, Wilkinson was dead. Twenty minutes later the ship broke up.

However, the rocket crew arrived at about 4.30 in the afternoon while the crew were still on the ship, and although the first line fired broke, the second line set up by H. Morris, a farmer at Barruppa, crossed the ship and was made fast. The chair had not arrived and as the tide rose, the men decided to come ashore along the line, and as it sagged some were washed off. They swam the line. It had as many as five men moving hand over hand for the beach where they were

43

rescued by men who threw off their clothes and raced into the surf to reach them before they were swept away. Yet, ten were washed off and drowned.

Of the survivors, only six were able to climb the cliff to Rivernook and the remainder camped on the beach, warming themselves at fires made from the wreckage. Next morning, they too reached shelter, where they remained for some time.

A day or two after the wreck it was declared that Wilkinson was alive when the last man left the ship. When his battered body was recovered his hands were clenched around straws and wooden matches, which gave rise to the belief that he may have clutched them when struggling for the shore after the ship broke up. Against this assertion, Captain Vickers claimed that he had carefully examined the young man who was undoubtedly dead. He explained the presence of straw and matches in the dead man's hands by the fact that when taken on board he was laid on an old straw mattress, and that there were matches where he lay. The carpenter stated that although Wilkinson was at first delirious and later unconscious, he believed that this occurred when he struck his head on the anchor chains just before they were both pulled from the water.

Strong criticism was levelled through the press at the complete failure of the sea rescue attempts, and the comparative failure of those by land. The Warrnambool lifeboat did not arrive, the Government steamer, LADY LOCH, reached the scene a day too late and the tug, RACER, started for the wreck but also failed to arrive. The lifesaving gear left Port Campbell late in the afternoon in two buggies; the first containing the tripod and four rockets; the second the heavy rope and chair. The two buggies became separated at the Gellibrand River crossing, and although the first buggy containing the rocket gear reached the wreck and a line was soon fired over the FIJI, many believed that the delay with the rope and chair contributed to the deaths of the men lost when attempting to come ashore along the line. Others wondered how a well-known Warrnambool photographer, who was holidaying at Port Campbell, had been able to transport his bulky camera gear to the scene while half the rocket apparatus was supposedly held up at the river.

At this time a regular gang of wreckers and smugglers was established in the Western District, who, though nominally small settlers, practised many acts of lawlessness including illicit distilling. It was in connection with the wreck of the FIJI that they first came under notice of the Customs. Some loaded up horses and buggies with booty taken from the beaches after the ship broke up. It included cases of brandy, gin, toys, pianos and cakes of dynamite. Drunken men roamed the countryside offering bottles of stolen liquor to strangers, and a rumour swept the district that the ship had carried jewellery. One Customs Officer attempting to protect the cargo, intercepted a group of men removing packages. He was assaulted and thrown over a steep cliff, but managed to cling to a bush about fifty feet down, until rescued.

Other local residents seized large quantities of whisky and other spirits as they floated ashore, burying cases and casks in the sandhills. Some is believed still buried in remote gullies, lost when the sands shifted.

One settler, Bill Skinner, of Chapple Vale, was near death when news of the FIJI reached his ears. At his insistence, sorrowing relatives took him to the beach where he soon joined the festivities occasioned, no doubt, by the broaching of a few flasks of whisky, brandy and rum. When he couldn't drink any more he said, "Pour it over me boys, I love it." Bill lived for many more years.

Pupils attending the small school near Lower Gellibrand arrived at school one morning soon after the wreck, to find the teacher dressed in his holiday clothes. "Holiday today children", he announced. "I'm off to the wreck today to do a little fossicking in the sand, and if I find what I'm looking for, you'll probably have a holiday for a couple more days."

The continuous heavy seas which roll in on to Wreck Beach prevented organised salvage attempts but in 1894, F. Clarke of Cobden purchased the wreck which by this time, was partly sanded over and lying in twenty feet of water. He engaged several divers who managed to salvage some of the hundreds of tons of coiled wire rope which had formed part of her cargo.

At the Court of Marine Inquiry, James Campbell, Second Mate, the officer in charge of the vessel at the time she struck, could give no explanation as to why the FIJI went ashore. The compasses were correct and the usual observations had been made the day before. At the time of the disaster the ship was under nearly all sail, the weather was squally and hazy, but the Cape Otway light was in sight.

However, Captain Vickers was severely reprimanded for his incompetent handling of the ship and his Master's Certificate was suspended for twelve months.

The Court found:
1. The courses set after sighting Cape Nelson were not safe and proper as no allowance was made for leeway and southerly swell.
2. The wreck could not be attributed to any unusual tide or current.
3. The master neglected to take soundings, and after the Otway light was sighted, was not sufficiently prompt in putting the ship about.

Two of the ship's apprentices, Ernest Lecky and Louis Evans, remained in the district for some time after the wreck. Lecky, an Irishman, aged 19, described his reactions when the ship struck. He was in his bunk and mistook the shock for the dropping of the anchor at Port Phillip Heads. When the alarm was given he put on his trousers, ran on deck, and remained waiting with the rest of the crew until the life line was fired aboard. When on the line, half-way to shore, his strength began to fail, but the Second Mate, a short distance behind, managed to shove him through the surf until his feet touched bottom.

45

One of the young women who helped care for the survivors, Miss A. Bowker, later Mrs R. Webster, of Colac, corresponded with Gebauhr's family for many years and followed the young sailor's career with great interest. Gebauhr joined a ship in Melbourne in 1892 and left Australia. In 1898 he rescued a seaman who fell overboard in the South Atlantic and was decorated by the German Kaiser. He became a Captain at 25 and spent his later years as a marine expert, in which capacity he toured the world, retiring in 1950 and dying at his home in Jersey City, U.S.A. in April 1956, aged 81.

NEWFIELD – 1892

Built at Dundee in Scotland in 1889. 1,386 tons. Length, 248.6 feet; beam, 35.3 feet; depth, 21.6 feet.

The barque NEWFIELD left Liverpool on June 1st with a cargo of fine rock salt for Brisbane and ran into very heavy weather approaching the Australian coast about six weeks later.

At about 9 p.m. on the night of August 29th, her master, Captain Scott, observed the Cape Otway light between heavy squalls, but due apparently to a compass error mistook it for the light on Cape Wickham, King Island, some forty miles to the south. Two hours later he altered course to the north-east, expecting to run through the western entrance to Bass Strait, but instead, his ship ran ashore at 3.40 a.m. about one mile east of Curdie's River.

The vessel struck heavily three times before grounding on an inner shoal with six feet of water in the holds.

The lifeboats were prepared, and the first launched containing two seamen and two apprentices was smashed against the side of the vessel before being swept away. One occupant, Levitt, regained the ship, while another, McLeod, was discovered some hours later crouched on a narrow ledge a few feet above sea level and hauled to safety.

After the first boat disappeared, the crew worked frantically for nearly an hour to launch the second, but a rising sea swept the decks making their work extremely dangerous. Twenty-three men crowded into the boat, but the lines entangled and it was pounded against the ship's side, sinking to the gunwales while the men clawed frantically at the smooth sides of the barque in an attempt to regain the deck.

One of the first to die was the boatswain, Dowse, who had been injured about a fortnight earlier and could scarcely move. He fell between the lifeboat and the NEWFIELD and was crushed, his body being recovered on the beach later in the day.

The cook, Jones, managed to regain the ship, and when he was joined by others, ropes and ladders were lowered to those struggling in the sea.

When all but six, including the Captain, had been dragged back on deck the ropes holding the lifeboat snapped and it was swept away, drowning the occupants.

Captain Scott, who had a share in the NEWFIELD, had worked his way from an ordinary seaman up to a Captain and intended to retire after the voyage. He was regarded by his crew as a thoroughly capable seaman although a very strict disciplinarian. The fact that he was disliked by several was admitted at the inquest into the deaths held later.

The First Mate, Sampson, took charge of the sixteen survivors and a third boat later landed with eight men, although it capsized when returning to the ship for the remainder and was lost.

The Port Campbell rocket crew arrived and fired four rockets, all of which went wide and further attempts were abandoned.

The Mate then lowered the one remaining boat, and after many anxious moments, all the crew landed safely, a man, Peter Carmody, swimming out through the surf with a lifeline from the rocket apparatus, to guide the boat ashore.

When word was received at Warrnambool the steamer JULIA PERCY, was hurriedly requisitioned to tow the lifeboat to the scene. On board JULIA PERCY was a police inspector, 3 constables, several customs officials and Doctor Scott. The lifeboat was rowed through heavy seas to make a closer inspection of the ship, but when it was seen that she was deserted except for the Captain's brown retriever and two pigs, she returned to Warrnambool.

The news that the cargo consisted of salt was a great disappointment to the hundreds who gathered on the cliffs, anticipating plunder similar to that taken from the FIJI less than twelve months earlier, but police were stationed on the beach to protect any valuables which washed ashore.

The NEWFIELD remained upright on the reef with sails set for a considerable time, as the wind slowly ripped the canvas to shreds and the sea battered the hull to pieces.

The Court of Marine Inquiry found as follows:

1. The NEWFIELD was properly equipped with charts and compasses.
2. Boats were sufficient and seaworthy but the skids on which they rested were rusty and stiff which hampered their launching in an emergency.
3. The ship carried sufficient life saving appliances but they were stored badly, and the master did not order their distribution when the ship struck.
4. The lead was not used for four hours prior to the stranding.
5. The master did not confer with his officers and it appeared that he kept the navigation of the vessel exclusively in his own hands.
6. A proper lookout was kept and the light and land was reported to the master.

From the evidence the master was blamed for the stranding. Throughout the voyage he did not appear to have consulted his officers as to the navigation of the ship.

FREETRADER – 1894

Built 1850. 188 tons. Length, 111 feet; beam, 22.2 feet; depth, 11 feet.

"The roughest voyage I ever had in my life", remarked Captain Bowden when his vessel, the FREETRADER, arrived in Lady Bay from New Zealand with a cargo of 160,000 feet of timber for P.J. McGennan of Warrnambool. The FREETRADER had encountered gales throughout the entire voyage and was almost lost when the wind veered as she entered the bay, only the skill of Pilot Drewett prevented disaster. However, Captain Bowden's troubles were only just beginning.

After unloading, the ship was preparing to depart for Newcastle when more rough weather delayed her sailing. She appeared safely anchored when one cable parted and she began to drift towards the mouth of the Hopkins River. A second anchor was let go, but when it also parted, the vessel drifted rapidly towards the shore, dragging the only remaining anchor, a small kedge.

Despite the frantic efforts of the crew, she struck broadside on to the piling which carried pipes connecting with the swimming baths, and in a short time they had battered a hole in the hull through which the water poured in an uncontrollable stream. Captain Bowden rushed to his cabin to save papers and personal effects but rising water forced him to abandon his efforts. Blue lights were burned to attract attention, but Captain and crew had little trouble scrambling over the piling to the shore, the Captain and his son, who was Mate, being the last to leave.

Bowden and his son were billeted at the Prince of Wales Hotel, and the crew went to the Bay View Hotel. The FREETRADER lay in about four feet of water at low tide, about midway between the remains of the ENTERPRISE and the OLIVIA DAVIS. She was later dismantled.

Captain Bowden who lost everything had been in charge of the barque for about eight years.

The Court of Marine Inquiry investigating the wreck found that the stranding was attributable to stress of weather, and no blame was attached to the Captain or officers.

INVERLOCHY – 1902

Built in Glasgow in 1895. 1,339 tons. Length, 238.5 feet; beam, 36 feet; depth, 21.7 feet.

The three-masted iron barque INVERLOCHY inward bound from Liverpool ran onto the Ingoldsby or Hereford Reef off Point Roadknight, Anglesea, on December 18th.

The vessel under the command of Captain Kendricks, an old officer in the famous Loch Line, left Liverpool on September 10th with 2,809 tons of general cargo and had an uneventful voyage until Cape Otway was sighted.

Split Point lighthouse was passed in very calm conditions and soon after the lookout, Thomas Steele, called "breakers ahead". The master attempted to tack and wear the vessel, but she grounded just as anchors were dropped.

About half an hour later the Chief Officer and ten men took a boat ashore but the Captain, his wife, one officer and ten men remained for several hours.

When they finally left they were forced east by prevailing winds and were forced to maintain a fixed course to avoid being swamped. Blue lights were fired in an endeavour to attract attention, but finally the occupants landed about one mile west of Barwon Heads.

The Queenscliff lifeboat and the Split Point Lighthouse keepers, equipped with rockets, travelled to the wreck but were not required.

Later, four Anglesea men rowed out in calm weather and furled the sails, while local men were also employed patrolling the beach to protect the revenue before the hull was sold for £320.

The vessel remained fast on the edge of the reef in about 18 feet of water and it soon became apparent that she was settling and warping badly. Most of the cargo was recovered and salvage men used divers during the removal of fittings.

She eventually became a total wreck, and for many years her figurehead stood on the Esplanade at Torquay and her bell hung on the verandah of the Anglesea Hotel.

The list of her cargo gives an excellent picture of the type of goods imported into Australia early in the century.

Slag, Boracic Acid, Borax, Carbonate of Soda, Cotton Waste, Wire Rope, Alum, Whisky, Glue, Steel, Cordage, Fire Bricks, Tiles, Yarn Twine, Hoop Iron, Stout, Pig Iron, Silicate of Soda, Furniture, Mangles, Beer, Tin Boxes, Casks, Rum, Brandy, Earthenware, Cyanide, Calcium, Soap, Paint, Magnesia, Oil Cloth.

It is interesting to note that the Court of Marine Inquiry held in Melbourne was terminated when a point of law was raised concerning the legality of the Marine Act.

Captain Kendricks was found guilty of misconduct by the Melbourne Court, had his certificate suspended for twelve months and was ordered to pay £120 towards the expenses of the investigation.

LA BELLA – 1905

A three-masted barquentine, built in Norway in 1893. 406 tons. Length, 144 feet; beam, 27.3 feet; depth, 12.5 feet.

Early in the evening of November 10th, LA BELLA, fully loaded with a cargo of timber from New Zealand, struck rocks south of the Warrnambool breakwater.

Most of the lifeboat crew were away at Port MacDonnell, but a volunteer crew was soon organised and the lifeboat taken out to the wreck which was lying on its beam ends taking a terrific battering from the heavy seas.

For more than an hour they attempted to rescue the crew lashed to the rail, but after repeated failure, returned to the pier to collect the rocket gear which was then mounted in the lifeboat. However, several attempts to fire a rocket aboard failed, and as the ship began to slip into deep water, the crew commenced their frantic battle for life.

A local fisherman, William Ferrier, displayed great courage when he sculled his small dinghy out twice close under the doomed vessel and rescued two men, one of whom was the Captain. Others were picked up by the lifeboat but altogether, only five of the crew of twelve were saved.

Ferrier, who was 25 years of age when he carried out his daring rescue, was awarded the Silver Medal of the Royal Humane Society. His son, Frank, received a similar award almost fifty years later, when he helped rescue four members of the crew of the yacht MERLAN, after it ran on to a reef near the Point Lonsdale Lighthouse.

The Court of Marine Inquiry found the master, Captain Mylius, guilty of careless navigation, suspended his certificate for twelve months, and ordered him to pay £28 towards the expense of the investigation.

This is his report on the disaster:

"The atmosphere was hazy and there was a heavy south-west sea running. The helmsman was ordered to steer for the light, but while the ship was coming round, a tremendous sea struck her on the port quarter, and she broached to, heading north-west. The helm was then put hard up and the vessel began to slowly pay off, when another breaking sea struck her on the port quarter and threw her broadside on to the swell. She again gathered way and began to pay off, when the First Mate on the forecastle reported breakers ahead. Shortly after, the ship struck and remained fast with heavy seas breaking over her. The boats were ordered to be got out, but they were at once filled and broken, and the crew were forced to take to the rigging. The vessel at first listed to starboard, but at 10 p.m. righted herself after the foremast went. At 11 p.m. three of the crew left their places in the fore rigging to take shelter in the foreward deckhouse, which was shortly after gutted by the sea, and they were not seen again. Two others from the crew became unconscious from exhaustion about midnight and were lashed to the rail, but at 2 a.m. they were washed away. At 7 a.m. the ship turned broadside to the sea. The First mate, who had his leg injured, and a boy, were too weak to hold on any longer and were washed away. After consulting with the Second Mate, I advised the men remaining to take to the water as the vessel was breaking up fast. The Second Mate swam to the lifeboat about 250 yards distant. Myself, having an injured foot and arm, swam to Mr Ferrier's punt, and the other two men swam to the lifeboats which had approached closer, and the last man was hauled off with a line.

Signed: Geo. Mylius. Master."

FALLS OF HALLADALE – 1908

Built in Glasgow in 1886. 2,085 tons. Length, 275.2 feet; beam, 41.6 feet; depth, 23.9 feet.

When the barques FALLS OF HALLADALE and FALLS OF GARRY were completed in 1886, they were the first vessels equipped with lifting fore and aft bridges which enabled the crew to move over the entire deck in heavy weather and remain safe and dry.

The FALLS OF HALLADALE was built for carrying capacity more than speed and her square bilge earned her the name of a "warehouse type" of ship. She carried no yards on her jigger mast, but thirty four foot yards for skysails on main and mizzen masts, one hundred and eighty feet above her decks, while her lower yards of eighty-two feet were shorter than usual on a 2,000 ton barque of that time.

However, she had one advantage; she could carry full sail safely without endangering her masts in the heaviest gale, and this is what was almost needed to drive her at 13 knots or make a run of 300 miles in 24 hours. She spent most of her life in the Pacific grain trade and her slowness or care of sails caused her to be posted missing or overdue on several occasions.

In 1893 on a voyage from Tyne to San Francisco with a cargo of bricks, coke, and pig iron she struck head winds from the north of Scotland to the Equator, then, after taking four weeks to battle around Cape Horn, ran into light winds in the Pacific. This voyage occupied 187 days.

Her worst passage was in 1903–04 when, after sailing from Liverpool in July, she was badly battered for three weeks trying to round Cape Horn, losing nineteen sails and leaking badly. Then, one night during a storm, most of the deck work, including the bridges, was smashed by a great sea forcing Captain Thomson to turn her around and run east around the Cape of Good Hope. The crew were becoming mutinous before the vessel reached Invercargill, New Zealand, on New Year's Day, 1904. After the barque set sail once again, seven seamen were put in irons, but she finally reached San Francisco in March 1904, after a voyage of 238 days, missing her main royal mast, mizzen royal yard, and most fittings bent or damaged.

Other slow voyages were, Mission Bay to Grimsby in 130 days; San Francisco to Queenstown in 172 days; Astoria to Queenstown in 169 days.

The FALLS OF HALLADALE left New York late in 1908 with a general cargo for Melbourne and Sydney which included roofing slates, benzine, paper, plaster, oysters, lubricating oil, wire, stoves, resin, glucose, clocks, medicine, timber and a variety of small items. On the night of November 14th, Captain Thomson estimated her to be off the Victorian coast, travelling at about six knots before a light breeze. He was uncertain of his correct position as a heavy fog had reduced visibility to less than 400 yards, and when the fog lifted slightly revealing high cliffs he realised he was too close in but was unable to save the ship in the light conditions. The FALLS OF HALLADALE grounded on a reef west of Peterborough and after a short delay the crew of 29 got clear in the boats and landed safely.

The ship, firmly wedged between two reefs with all sail set, attracted hundreds of sightseers over a period of nearly two months until heavy seas and the dynamiting of salvagers reduced her to a total wreck. The first venture was a financial failure as was a second attempt about twelve months later.

After the wreck, the Second Mate, Mr T. Griffin, took up land near Peterborough, and on the outbreak of war in 1914 enlisted, taking part in the Gallipoli campaign before being invalided to England and later discharged. He returned to Peterborough and later resided at Banool and Colac, where he remained until his death in June 1956.

Captain Thomson was found guilty by a Court of Marine Inquiry of a gross act of misconduct in that he carelessly navigated the ship by neglecting to take proper soundings, and by failing to place the ship on the port tack before it became too late to do so. His certificate was suspended for six months and he was ordered to pay £15-15-0 toward inquiry expenses.

During the inquiry several controversial matters were discussed:

1. About three-quarters of an hour before the ship ran aground the helmsman, Willian Nixey, saw land, but failed to report it, believing he would be reprimanded if he did so.
2. When the boatswain and Second Mate reported sighting land to the Captain about 30 minutes later, he seemed undecided on his future actions and returned to the chart room to consult his chart.
3. After the ship struck in the early hours of the morning confusion reigned. Boats were manned and the captain left without securing the ship's papers. He said he thought they were in one of the two bags he threw into the boat, but admitted he had not looked to see whether they were there.
4. The Court believed the master showed a lamentable lack of judgment and want of prompt decision, and these factors cost him the FALLS OF HALLADALE.
5. The Court also bluntly pointed out to the First Mate that he showed a want of intelligence and capacity in claiming that it was not a proper thing to take soundings on a sailing vessel, and an utter indifference to duty in saying there was too much to do on a sailing vessel to take soundings.

SPECULANT – 1911

Built 1895. Traded under the Russian flag until 1902. 393 tons gross; 363 tons net. Length, 150 feet; beam, 24 feet; depth, 11.4 feet.

One of the most spectacular sections of the Ocean Road winds effortlessly around the precipitous cliffs of Cape Patten, but when the barquentine SPECULANT was wrecked at its foot in 1911 only a rough track wound through the scrub near its summit.

In 1902 McGerran & Company, Box Nail and Barbed Wire manufacturers, purchased the SPECULANT in Great Britain for £3,000 and commissioned Captain Jacobson to sail her to Australia where she soon became known as the largest barquentine trading in Victorian waters, and also the largest vessel ever registered at Warrnambool.

She was sailing from Portland to Melbourne in ballast on February 10th, when driven ashore by a strong south-westerly gale on a voyage that had already taken three weeks, as she had been forced back on two occasions by rough weather.

The SPECULANT rounded Cape Otway in a heavy gale and misty conditions. Her Captain believed her to be well clear of land when a tremendous crash threw all off their feet. Heavy seas broke over the ship and she was dumped on jagged rocks and her bottom smashed in. The crew managed to fasten a line to a large rock a few yards from the ship and from here they climbed across to a second rock, before dragging themselves ashore. Apart from badly lacerated hands, they were uninjured. Believing Lorne to be the nearest settlement, the party of eight headed east, but with the coming daylight realised their mistake and retraced their steps.

When first seen by C. Ramsden, a local farmer, they were dressed in an assortment of underwear and night attire and were mistaken for escapees from a reformatory at that time being conducted by a Colonel Heath at Apollo Bay, but once their identity was established, he took them to the home of his brother, sheep and geese were killed and the sailors fed and decently clothed. There was only one Australian in the crew, but of the remainder, all Swedish, only the Captain could speak English.

Later, a few ventured back on to the wreck to retrieve a few personal belongings, but the ship remained firmly wedged in the rocks, being gradually battered to pieces by the heavy seas which break on the cape and visited at low tide by venturesome souvenir hunters.

The Court inquiring into the wreck found Captain Jacobson guilty of careless navigation by not taking steps to accurately verify the position of the vessel with respect to Cape Otway when the light was visible, and by not setting a safe and proper course with respect to the wind and sea. It suspended his certificate for six months and ordered him to pay £6 for the expense of the investigation.

Mr W.E. Ramsden presented the SPECULANT's bell to the Apollo Bay Surf Life Saving Club for use as a shark alarm in 1959, but unfortunately, it was stolen after about ten years' service.

ANTARES - 1914

Built in Glasgow in 1888 and originally named SUTLEJ. Bought in 1907 by Semider Brothers of Genoa, refitted and renamed ANTARES.

1,749 tons. Length, 260.3 feet; beam, 38.2 feet; depth, 23.1 feet.

The wreck of the ANTARES near Nullawarre in 1914 was overshadowed by war news, and passed almost unnoticed.

A district lad went home one night remarking that the Germans had arrived off the Victorian coast and he had seen and heard them firing shells and flares against the night sky, but his story was passed off as a joke.

About a month later, a local resident riding along the cliffs which tower sheer out of the sea more than 200 feet, saw what he thought were the remains of a ship. Police were notified and the Warrnambool lifeboat was sent to investigate.

The Warrnambool Harbour Master, Captain Marshall, reported that the wreck could be clearly seen in about eight feet of water. The spars were lying over one side and he was able to trace the outline of a ship which appeared to have been split open. He discovered the remains of a black man and a board bearing the name SUTLEJ. Wreckage was strewn along the base of the cliffs and it appeared her cargo consisted mainly of roofing tiles. The body recovered was buried in the Warrnambool cemetery, but there was no sign of the other twenty-four members of the crew.

3 – Steamers

Steamers first appeared on the Australian coast in 1831 and within a few years were a common sight in Victorian waters. In 1853 the paddle steamer MANCHESTER became the first regular vessel on the West Coast run, and she was followed by S.S. CHAMPION, LADY BIRD and QUEEN. Burning coal, the speed and range of these early vessels were limited, but once their engines were improved they soon replaced sail on all regular services.

CONSIDE – 1852

Built 1847. 259 tons. Length, 105.5 feet; beam, 26.9 feet; depth, 16.6 feet.

Just before midnight on September 14th, S.S. CONSIDE, Captain Appleby, a crew of 21, carrying 180 passengers, five horses and general cargo was apparently misled by lights on the schooner PORTLAND, wrecked a few hours earlier, and ran on to the Lonsdale Reef.

Immediately she struck, nineteen passengers panicked, rushed into one of the lifeboats, released only the stern fall and were precipitated into the sea. Only five regained the ship.

Next, a small group looted the cabin and passengers' luggage but Captain Appleby, the officers and some passengers succeeded in destroying the wines and spirits before they found it.

The Second Officer left the vessel to obtain help and early next morning S.S. MAITLAND rescued the survivors and took them on to Melbourne. Unfortunately the five horses perished.

After hanging to the rock for two days with her bow in deep water inside the reef, the vessel went to pieces.

CHAMPION – 1857

Built 1854. 229 tons. Length, 129.4 feet; beam; 21.2 feet; depth, 11.2 feet.

The screw steamer CHAMPION arrived at Portland from London via Perth and Adelaide on December 23rd, 1854, after being delayed in South Australian waters. When passing through the Backstairs Passage at night, she collided with P.S. MELBOURNE and damaged her so badly she was forced to tow her back to Adelaide.

With a top speed exceeding twelve knots, accommodation for 40 cabin and 60 steerage passengers, 200 tons of cargo and sufficient coal to steam for ten days without refuelling the CHAMPION was an immediate success.

On the night of August 24th, 1857, the CHAMPION steaming to Melbourne sighted S.S. LADY BIRD on the Melbourne side of Cape Otway in fine, calm conditions. Both were travelling at full speed and when close by both helms appeared to be ported and the vessels collided.

The stem of the LADY BIRD cut at least seventeen feet into the CHAMPION near the main mast cutting a gaping hole in the hull over the saloon. Most of her passengers were in bed and the loss of life was heavy; thirty-two being drowned. As the vessels parted, Captain Helpman called for lifeboats which rescued people from spars and boxes. After searching for an hour the LADY BIRD returned to Geelong, passing through the Heads at 10 a.m. next morning. Only the forecastle bulkhead saved her from sinking as her bow plates were badly damaged along with her bowsprit and cutwater. Immediately after the collision, Captain White had her lightened up forward.

Survivors told many tragic stories. One passenger saw Mrs McKenzie endeavouring to save her two children in the sinking poop of the CHAMPION. Another, a Mr Le Souef was hanging onto the bowsprit of the LADY BIRD as the vessels parted. The Second Mate of the LADY BIRD rescued the stewardess of the CHAMPION and they were later married. A racehorse aboard the CHAMPION broke loose, swam seven miles to the shore and raced again in the Western District.

When the LADY BIRD reached Melbourne, her passengers drew up a testimonial praising Captain White for his conduct and handling of the vessel during and after the collision.

The Steam Navigation Board held an inquiry a fortnight later and found that the Masters of both vessels were guilty of want of action and non enforcement of discipline, and that the Chief Officers of both vessels were guilty of neglect of duty and recklessness, but recorded an open finding. The widow of one of the passengers who drowned in the CHAMPION sued the owners and was awarded substantial damages.

Captain Helpman at the inquiry, said that he was resting in his cabin when he heard the Mate call "Port". Rushing on deck he saw the other vessel and immediately ordered "hard-a-port" and "full speed". The vessel did not respond and the collision occurred with the CHAMPION sinking almost immediately.

The evidence of Andrew Hutchinson, a fore cabin passenger on the CHAMPION, gives some indication of the suddenness of the disaster. "I embarked at Port Fairy about noon on Monday. I was below when the collision took place. The concussion roused me. No one called out, to my knowledge. I was lying on one of the berths when I heard the shock.

"Someone said, 'It's only the chain down,' but I made for the deck. One of the CHAMPION's sailors cried out, 'For God's sake lower the boats', and suspecting something was wrong I rushed aft. When I found myself in the water I swam off and was taken hold of by another. I secured an oar and was picked up in an exhausted state by one of the boats."

ANT - 1866

Built 1854. 149 tons. Length, 100.8 feet; beam, 17.8 feet; depth, 9.2 feet.

A strong inshore current has been blamed for several wrecks in the vicinity of Bream Creek, and the small steamer ANT became one of the first recorded victims when it ran ashore on Tuesday, June 12th.

The ANT left Circular Head in Tasmania on June 11th, with nine passengers, a crew of seventeen, and a cargo of wheat, skins, potatoes, and sixteen sheep.

At daylight next morning, in the midst of a heavy fog, her master, Captain Harrison, estimated their position as being about midway between Cape Patten and Airey's Inlet and set a course to the east. After running for about ten miles, breakers were heard, and although the watch was doubled, engines set at half speed, and a course set to the south, the vessel struck a rock about five miles west from Barwon Heads.

Immediately, a seaman reported the fore compartment full of water, and the vessel could not be moved due to an engine failure.

Fortunately, the sea was moderate, there being a heavy roll but no break, enabling boats to be lowered immediately, but as the vessel did not appear in immediate danger, only one boat containing several passengers and crew members pushed off and remained clear of the roll about half a mile distant. Following a lengthy discussion concerning the passengers' luggage, all excepting the captain, chief steward, carpenter, and two passengers left the ship. However, about 10 a.m. the same morning the ANT filled with water, and broke her back, forcing those remaining on board to throw the sheep into the sea before taking to a boat.

A fishing boat took Captain Harrison on to Queenscliff and Captain Tulloch and three hands returned to the wreck to guard the cargo until the steamer, SAMSON, with a whaleboat in tow, arrived from Melbourne.

Captain Harrison attributed the wreck to a faulty steering compass.

Hopes were high that the ANT could be refloated, and 80 casks and two pumps were taken to the wreck to be placed in the hold to float her off, but the plan failed, leaving her hanging on the reef with her keel out of the water and her stern completely buried.

Before salvage work commenced, vandals visited the wreck and stole many fittings from the cabins.

An inquiry held on June 19th, found Captain Harrison guilty of negligence on the following charges:

1. Placing confidence in compasses which had been proved defective less than 18 hours earlier.
2. Navigating at full speed in a fog up to within a few minutes of the wreck.
3. Neglecting to take soundings.

BARWON – 1871

Built 1868. 419 tons. Length, 172.3 feet; beam, 21.6 feet; depth, 14 feet.

Coming around the coast to Portland, during a voyage from Adelaide to Sydney, loaded with flour, the BARWON struck a rock west of Cape Bridgewater during a heavy fog on April 3rd.

The sea was calm and her master, Captain Shoobert, decided to beach her in Bridgewater Bay. However, she sank before reaching the shore although her crew and 28 passengers reached safety in her boats.

An inquiry conducted by the Steam Navigation Board found Captain Shoobert and the Second Mate guilty of a number of charges. Shoobert lost his Master's Certificate for three months.

NAPIER – 1878

Built 1874. 98 tons. Length, 120.6 feet; beam, 17 feet; depth, 8.6 feet.

Chartered to work the wreck of the LOCH ARD, she ran on to rocks in Port Campbell Bay on September 16th, and became a total loss.

Her master, Captain Limschow, inspected Port Campbell inlet before commencing salvage work, and was satisfied it would provide a reasonably safe anchorage in rough weather.

On her second trip she lost an anchor and chain and was forced to return to Geelong. Then, when she returned on September 16th, the sea was high, forcing her to take shelter in the tiny inlet.

She entered along the eastern side, but as she swung in the tiny bay, the swell forced her on to rocks, holding her up forward and lifting the stern on to a shelf, breaking one of her twin propellors and portion of the tiller. Then, in attempting to kedge her clear, two boats were damaged. Two divers who examined her believed she could be repaired and refloated, but after everything removeable had been recovered, and she lay waiting for a pump to arrive from Warrnambool, another gale destroyed her. Rough seas battered six more holes in her and she was abandoned by captain and crew, leaving ten men and a diver to dismantle as much as possible before she went to pieces. Portion of her boiler may still be seen opposite the jetty at low tide.

BLACK BOY - 1883

(See wreck of George Roper, page 35.)

SELJE - 1929

Built at Sunderland in 1921. 6,598 tons. Length, 420 feet; beam, 54 feet; depth, 34 feet.

Homeward bound from Melbourne to Norway with 114,000 bags of wheat in the holds, most of the crew of the Norwegian freighter SELJE were relaxing in their bunks on the night of March 30th, when the bow of the steamship KAITUNA sliced a huge hole about sixty feet from the stern.

Originally named HALLGRIM, the SELJE was a steamship with oil fired boilers, registered at Bergen, Norway, and at the time of the collision proceeding at about nine knots to Las Palmas in the Canary Islands, for further orders.

The British steamship KAITUNA, master A. Sizer, registered at Dunedin, New Zealand, was travelling between Adelaide and Melbourne with a crew of 31 and general cargo.

The collision occurred at 10.05 p.m. a few miles south-west of Cape Otway in clear weather, with a light southerly wind and moderate swell.

Captain Endressen, who was accompanied by his wife, realised immediately that the ship was sinking and ordered the launching of two lifeboats. In the swell both were swept against the side of the ship, one being badly damaged, but the crew managed to get clear in the second, although it was taking water. When all 32 of the crew were in the lifeboat, the captain jumped into the sea and was later taken into the lifeboat.

The SELJE sank twenty minutes after the collision, the radio officer remaining at his post almost to the last. As he jumped into the sea and clambered into the lifeboat, it swamped and all baled desperately to remain afloat.

The KAITUNA standing by 100 yards away launched boats and threw rope ladders which the crew used to climb aboard. The KAITUNA herself was badly damaged with her bows stove in and several bad leaks near the waterline, but, after a short delay tarpaulins were fastened around the leaks and over her bows, enabling her to limp towards Melbourne.

The tug EAGLE met her outside the Heads, but she continued under her own steam to Williamstown, and later Victoria Dock.

The Court of Marine Inquiry found that the KAITUNA was to blame for the collision, but praised both masters for their conduct. A charge of negligence against the Third Mate who was officer in charge of the watch on the KAITUNA was not sustained.

CASINO – 1932

Built 1882. 425 tons. Length, 160.4 feet; beam, 24.1 feet; depth, 10.2 feet.

Apollo Bay's worst shipping disaster occurred just after 9 a.m. on Sunday, July 10th, when the old coastal steamer CASINO capsized and sank in heavy seas about a quarter of a mile off shore.

The CASINO arrived from England in May 1882, on her delivery voyage to New South Wales, where she was to enter the coastal trade, and while coaling at Warrnambool was almost blown ashore near where the OLIVIA DAVIS had been wrecked a few weeks earlier. Captain Wilson was ashore interviewing the agents when the wind changed, causing her to drag her anchor almost into the surf. Prompt action by the pilot resulted in the anchor cable being cut and the vessel headed out to sea.

Shortly after, in July, she was purchased by the Belfast and Koroit Steam Navigation Company for £14,250, and operated around the south-western Victorian coast calling at Portland, Port Fairy, Warrnambool and later Apollo Bay. In addition to passengers she carried wool, meat, butter and many essential items. Having made about 2,500 trips on the one run, her record was unequalled by any other coastal steamer.

Originally, she had three masts but one was removed. In her early days she was rigged as a topsail schooner and her big spread of canvas helped to keep down fuel consumption. Burning coal, and later briquettes, and with a spread of sail the CASINO showed a surprising turn of speed. Unless the weather was bad she hugged the coast, providing her passengers with magnificent views of the rugged cliffs, particularly those in the Port Campbell area.

Three highlights in her fifty-year career occurred in 1915, 1924 and 1929. In 1915 she collided with the BATMAN off Point Gellibrand, but both vessels suffered only minor damage. In 1924 she ran ashore on a reef off Point Hawdon near the Grey River. The tug EAGLE was sent to her assistance but she could not be freed until most of her cargo had been unloaded or dumped into the sea. Leaking badly she returned to Melbourne under her own steam, leaving workmen from a large road camp to enjoy the beer and spirits which made up part of her cargo. One night in February, 1929, during a power blackout at Warrnambool, she attempted to enter Lady Bay when points of identification were difficult to locate and was almost safely in the harbour when she struck a submerged object, rapidly filled with water and developing a dangerous list. Soundings showed twelve feet of water in the holds, and she was beached near Bay View until temporary repairs enabled her to return to Melbourne, still listing badly.

Apollo Bay lies in one of the most treacherous parts of the Victorian coast, and often mountainous seas rise without warning, receding almost as suddenly. On many occasions the CASINO would be forced to by-pass the port or stand off for calmer weather, and on other occasions, heavy mooring ropes were snapped and bollards torn from the ship's deck.

On the morning of July 10th, the CASINO, carrying a crew of 17, two passengers, about 240 tons of cargo, mostly sugar, and drawing about 11 ft. 6 in. of water, attempted to berth at the long Apollo Bay pier.

She approached the 1000-foot pier at about half tide, falling into the troughs of the long rollers whipped up by the south-easterly gale that had been lashing the coast for two days. As the vessel manoeuvred to draw in to the pier, the bottom struck the sand several times with a jarring thud that shook the vessel from stem to stern. Although the impacts were so severe that they threw the crew in the engine room off their feet, they were not alarmed, as this had happened during storms on several occasions.

Captain John Middleton ordered the engines stopped, and for about half an hour, efforts were made to manoeuvre the CASINO alongside the pier.

When about 100 yards out the vessel was slewed around to the east so as to go in stern first, and when the stern was about 40 yards from the jetty, the port anchor was dropped. The Chief Officer let the anchor go, and the vessel swung on the anchor as was customary, heading at this time in the direction from which the wind was blowing. The head was then brought around so as to bring the starboard side alongside the jetty after going astern.

Two severe seas were shipped during this time and the vessel bumped at least four times. Although the CASINO had drawn closer to the jetty, she was not close enough in for the Second Officer to throw a line across.

The captain then decided to draw off the pier and anchor in deep water until the sea abated. He shouted down to the engine room, "I cannot make the jetty, I'm going out."

An order was given to pick up the anchor but it became fouled and was not released for some time. Watchers noted that the port anchor, weighing about 15 cwt. had been damaged, but neither captain nor crew realised that the vessel was taking in water at the bow until the centre of the bay was reached. Purser Stretton said later that the water was heard rushing into the hold and all realised that the ship was foundering.

Captain Middleton decided to beach her and immediately she was put about. To the watchers on shore, it was obvious she would not make the beach. The engine room crew were ordered on deck, the lifeboats were readied, and all prepared to abandon ship.

The Chief Engineer, Mr W. Newlands, described the wreck as "amazingly sudden". "When Captain Middleton gave the order to beach the ship," he said, "I kept the engines going full ahead until we were nearing the shore. The steam pumps were unable to cope with the water, which was rising rapidly in the hold, but the engine room staff stuck to their tasks until ordered on deck. I clung to the rigging, and as the ship heeled over I tried to help a man in the water near me. A great wave swept over the ship and washed me away. I seized a piece of handrail which carried me to the breakers. I believe that the loss of life would have been averted had it been possible to keep the engines running a few minutes longer, as by that time the ship could have beached."

Within two minutes of the order to launch lifeboats, the vessel had turned on her side and foundered. The stewardess, Mrs Gill, had fitted lifebelts to Mrs H. Convery of Apollo Bay and twelve-year-old Joan Greer of Portland, who were then placed in a lifeboat. One lifeboat jammed in its davits and the only two launched capsized immediately, throwing passengers into the water. The end followed quickly. The vessel heeled over and sank, throwing all aboard into the sea. All but five attempted to swim ashore. Eight of these made the beach and were rescued by residents of Apollo Bay, but Captain Middleton and four others struck back to the hull and succeeded in scrambling onto it. They signalled for assistance, but all efforts to reach them failed. As the tide rose, they were washed off and with one exception, drowned.

At about 8.45, Constable Malcolm Mildren received a phone call advising that the CASINO was in trouble. He informed the captain of the rocket corps and then hurried to the beach. Survivors were coming ashore and efforts were being made to resuscitate bodies washed into the surf.

Blankets, hot water bottles and first aid equipment was hurried to the beach, and those rescued were soon made comfortable in hotels and boarding houses in the town.

Mr F. Martin, of Apollo Bay, mounted a horse, rose out into the surf and was instrumental in rescuing several people. Messrs A. Fisk and J. Ley made repeated efforts to swim out with ropes, but the sea was too strong. Mr Martin was awarded the Royal Humane Society's silver medal for his part in the rescue and the efforts of several others were recognised by the society.

The lifesaving crew attempted to fire rockets to the ship, but had little success. The first line fired out snapped, and others went wide. When the lines were recovered and readied for firing again they became so heavy with water that the rockets could not carry them out against the strong wind. The men battling aboard the stricken ship clung desperately to the upturned hull as the tide rose. One by one they were washed off and drowned with one exception, cabin boy, R. Bellairs. The last man disappeared at about 12 noon. All that day and night a small party of volunteers under the direction of Constable Mildren, patrolled the beach finding nothing but splintered superstructure and decking.

Next day the sand was littered with wrecked fittings, furnishings including the new red plush cushions provided in the saloon to mark the 50th anniversary of her running on the Victorian coast, and scraps from the cargo.

There were many personal tragedies. Michael Foley, aged 20, and his father, Michael senr., aged 42, were together on the vessel. The son survived but his father was lost. The death of able seaman Peter Murray left eleven children fatherless. The stewardess, Helena Gill, aged 53, had served on the vessel for 23 years.

Captain Middleton went part of the way to shore grasping a plank. He reached the surf exhausted but collapsed and died before being taken from the water.

Wiltshire, the only survivor of the three firemen, was in a lifeboat with the cook, Kilpatrick, when it capsized. He grasped the First Mate by the collar but the sea tore him from his grasp. Wiltshire grabbed a window frame from the ship and was carried ashore. Peter Wiltshire was a fireman in the KOORINGA when it caught fire and exploded in Bass Strait in 1926, while carrying a full cargo of petrol and oil. He was one of the last to leave the stricken vessel and suffered severe burns.

Bellairs and Murray were the last two left on the ship as the tide rose. "I'm going to swim for it", Bellairs said. He was half-way to shore when picked up.

Mrs Convery floated part way to shore on a wooden box and completed the journey on a piece of timber when the case was washed away. Her husband, who was working on a farm directly above the bay, when he saw the CASINO sink, jumped onto his horse and dashed down to the beach, arriving as his wife crawled from the surf.

Four of the regular crew were on annual leave and had been replaced by temporary men. Binnie, the first officer, was formerly the ship's captain.

The CASINO was insured with Lloyd's of London for £12,000, three-quarters of her value.

A considerable amount of the cargo washed ashore and then "disappeared", despite the vigilance of police and officials, although some offenders were detected and fined.

A plane that flew over the wreck shortly after the tragedy noted that the funnel and both masts had disappeared and the upper deck works and bridge had been carried away. The vessel appeared to be settling on the edge of a sandbank.

Diver J. Johnstone inspected the ship on July 13th, and reported that it was lying on its port side in 22 feet of water with its stern to the beach about 400 yards out. He examined the bottom plates and rivets but found no damage. However, by the action of the water there appeared to be a fracture on the port side and the anchor was broken.

Later at the Colac Court House, Mr D.W. O'Grady, P.M., found that those lost died by drowning due to misadventure owing to the steamer being wrecked at Apollo Bay on July 10th.

The judgment of the Court of Marine Inquiry handed down on August 23rd, 1932, recorded the following:

1. The CASINO was wrecked at Apollo Bay on July 10th, 1932, at 8.44 a.m. through fouling the anchor when off the jetty and when manoeuvring from an anchorage, after the captain had decided that

weather conditions and the rough sea did not permit him to berth safely alongside the jetty. The stock of the anchor pierced the keel plate of the vessel abut 25 feet from the stem, making a hole nine inches in diameter. This caused a serious rush of water into the forehold of the vessel. Apparently the captain decided to immediately beach the vessel, but she sank at the head with a heavy list to port. With the stern out of the water, she became unmanageable and soon rolled over on her port side and sank broadside on to the breakers.

2. The vessel was seaworthy and carried regulation life saving appliances.

3. The vessel was navigated with proper and seamanlike care.

Many believed that had there been a lifeboat at Apollo Bay all would have been saved. Although it may not have been able to pull alongside the wreck to take the men off, it could have passed them a line.

The rocket equipment also came in for much adverse criticism being considered totally unsuitable and in poor condition.

The loss of the CASINO was a serious blow to the company, but the CORAMBA was purchased soon after, and continued in the trade for about two years until it was lost with all hands.

Another vessel was later used, but eventually road transport forced the company into liquidation.

Today, the CASINO still lies in the Apollo Bay harbour visited occasionally by skin divers and visible in fine, calm weather from Mariner's Lookout, north of the town.

The wheel and binnacle are in the Apollo Bay Hotel, and an anchor, lifebelts, and other relics may be found around the town. At Port Fairy a memorial cairn incorporating a bell and the ship's propeller recalls the tragedy.

CITY OF RAYVILLE – 1940

Built at Tampa, Florida, U.S.A., 1920. Converted to diesel 1927. 5,883 tons. Length, 401.9 feet; beam, 54.2 feet; depth, 31.2 feet.

Shortly after daybreak on November 9th, 1940, 37 members of the crew of the American freighter CITY OF RAYVILLE, wet and cold after sheltering in lifeboats in the choppy water of Bass Strait for more than 12 hours, stepped ashore at the tiny Victorian fishing port of Apollo Bay, situated close by the main shipping lanes and a few miles east of Cape Otway.

The CITY OF RAYVILLE, the second victim within 24 hours of an extensive minefield laid by German raiders about a fortnight earlier, was the first American vessel sunk in World War II.

The German raider PINGUIN, a motor vessel of 7766 tons, which had been sent to operate around the Australian coast during the winter months, and the Antarctic during the whaling season, disposed of 28 Allied vessels before she was destroyed by H.M.S. CORNWALL early in 1941.

On October 7th, 1940, when off the north-west coast of Australia, the Norwegian tanker STORSTAD was captured and the PINGUIN's captain, Ernst Kruder, decided this prize would be most useful as an additional minelayer, so after renaming her PASSAT and transferring the crew to his own ship, she was loaded with 110 mines and sailed to a point near North West Cape, Western Australia, where she spent three days undergoing conversion for minelaying.

Kruder had planned that his ships would mine the approaches to Sydney, Newcastle, Hobart, Adelaide and Melbourne before sailing south for general maintenance and overhaul, since the PINGUIN had been at sea six months.

On October 12th the PASSAT proceeded on a course parallel with the West Australian coast, passing Cape Leeuwin six days later and going southeast and around the south of Tasmania to the entrance of Banks Strait.

There, on the night of October 29th, she laid 30 mines in two lays, one of 5 and the other 25. Next night she passed east of Flinders Island and laid 30 mines in three fields of 10, between Deal and Cliffy Islands, in addition to 10 off Wilson's Promontory.

All that now remained was the western approaches near Cape Otway, where, on the night of October 31st, she laid 40 mines.

Immediately after the CITY OF RAYVILLE was lost, several Apollo Bay fishermen recalled that about a week earlier they had seen a large unidentified vessel while fishing at Point Franklin, a few miles east of Cape Otway.

This vessel had approached from the south, and when about two miles offshore, had turned and disappeared south-east. At the time the fishermen were puzzled by her movements, but the incident was forgotten and no report reached official circles.

A fortnight later the PASSAT rejoined the PINGUIN in the Indian Ocean. They continued operations together for a short time. When the PINGUIN was destroyed by the CORNWALL, her brave and resourceful captain went down with his ship.

The first victim of the minefields was the British steamer CAMBRIDGE (10,855 tons) as she rounded South East Point, Wilson's Promontory, some 2½ miles offshore at 11 p.m. on November 7th, 1940. The vessel sank rapidly, stern first, and of the complement of 58, one man, the carpenter, was lost. HMAS ORARA rescued the survivors and landed them at Welshpool.

Less than 24 hours later, at 7.30 p.m. on November 8th, the CITY OF RAYVILLE struck a mine six miles south of Cape Otway while bound from Adelaide to Melbourne, with 1500 tons of lead loaded at Port Pirie.

Local fishermen considered her extremely unlucky. The currents in the area reached four or five knots when the tide is running and any mines anchored to the sea bed would be dragged out of the perpendicular, thus clearing the shipping lane. The RAYVILLE, heavily laden and sitting low in the water, reached the area in slack water between tides when mines would provide the maximum hazard.

A bright flash, followed by the rumble of an explosion, alerted the Cape Otway lighthouse, which soon contacted Apollo Bay seeking help from the fishing fleet.

Conditions were not good. A strong north-easterly was whipping up the sea and most fishermen, anticipating bad weather, had winched their small craft, less than 30 feet in length, on to the pier, but three boats, owned by W. Ovens, T. Fisk and J. Muir, containing nine men, left immediately to search for survivors.

As the craft headed into the open sea on a search expected to take them more than 20 miles south of the port, they were swept by seas which necessitated constant bailing. In addition, rain squalls made observation difficult, but soon the fishermen were able to take bearings from the lighthouse, and some hours later flares were sighted about seven miles west from where the ship had sunk.

A long search in the darkness followed. Finally, after several false alarms, two lifeboats were located wallowing in the sea, lines were attached and they were towed back to Apollo Bay.

Later the ship's master, Captain Cronin, reported that the vessel had sunk in 35 minutes, bow first, the only casualty being the third engineer, M. Bryant, who had lost his life when he returned to the vessel to recover personal effects.

Bryant was seen to dive from the ship, but he apparently struck his head on floating debris and disappeared before the lifeboat could reach him.

The hotels in Apollo Bay generously cared for the Americans and the townspeople were lavish with their hospitality during the few days the crew spent in the port, where the men were clothed with the assistance of the Apollo Bay branch of the Red Cross.

Townspeople entertained the crew before their departure for Melbourne, while Lorne and Anglesea folk extended hospitality to them as they passed their towns. A few days later they were the guests of the Governor of Victoria, Sir Winston Dugan at Government House.

A delicate situation arose when the United States Consul General in Melbourne, after accepting an invitation to attend a dinner organised by the Otway Shire to honour the fishermen, withdrew at the last moment.

Several lengthy telephone calls and "straight talking" by the Shire Secretary, Tom Fry, restored the situation and the function proceeded as planned.

The illuminated address presented to the men is displayed in the Cable Station Museum, Apollo Bay.

The CITY OF RAYVILLE was the last vitim of the PASSAT's minefields. Soon afterwards a mine drifted ashore at Point Bunbury, on the edge of the town, where it was destroyed by naval men, and two were reported ashore at Station Beach, west of Cape Otway.

Minesweeping operations commenced on November 9th, and 43 mines from the Bass Strait fields were recovered by sweeping, destroyed after being found floating, or rendered safe after coming ashore. The last mine destroyed known to have come from the Cape Otway fields came ashore near Yuulong, west of Cape Otway, on December 11th, 1943.

The crew of the RAYVILLE returned to the U.S. and resumed service on American vessels, some being captured and killed by the Japanese.

Today, the CITY OF RAYVILLE still lies in about 200 feet of water, probably still intact. A reputed $34,000, pay for the crew in Melbourne, is locked in the strongroom, but to date no attempt has been made to salvage the cargo.

An Apollo Bay fisherman has the keys of the ship's strongroom, given to him by the captain, and also a letter which members of the rescue party received from the United States Government. It reads:

Washington,
January 22, 1941

My Dear Mr Stephens,

There has come to my attention your participation in the rescue of members of the crew of the American vessel CITY OF RAYVILLE off Cape Otway on the night of November 8, 1940.

On behalf of the President of the United States I wish to express to you his appreciation and that of this Government for your courageous and prompt action in going to the assistance of these American seamen.

Sincerely yours,

(Signed) CORDELL HULL, Secretary of State.

Another letter can be seen at Apollo Bay:

November 11, 1940

To the People of Apollo Bay,

Please accept the profound thanks and appreciation of the entire crew of the wrecked AM. US CITY OF RAYVILLE for the wonderful care and help extended to us when we were landed at Apollo Bay on the morning of November 9, 1940.

WALTER M. HART,
Chief Officer, US CITY OF RAYVILLE Motor Ship.

In a letter received early in May 1967, John E. Green supplied brief details of the subsequent careers of the ship's officers.

"I am presently Marine Superintendent of the Company who owned the RAYVILLE. After the sinking I returned to Australia a year later and was in Sydney on Pearl Harbour day, December 7th, 1941. I was sunk again by a German submarine off Durban, South Africa on March 8th, 1942, and spent 4 days in a lifeboat before being rescued.

"The Third Officer 'Hickey' is at present Master of one of the Company's North Atlantic vessels and the Fourth Officer 'Grande' is presently Director of the Company's Safety Programme."

ORUNGAL – 1940

Built at Glasgow, 1923. 5,826 tons. Length, 390.6 feet; beam, 55.2 feet; depth, 28.1 feet.

The S.S. ORUNGAL, owned by the Australian United Steam Navigation Company Limited, and commanded by Captain Gilling, left Sydney at midnight on November 19th with 16 passengers and 1,200 tons of general cargo, arriving off the Victorian coast next day.

The master accurately determined the ship's position at 11.38 a.m. on the 21st, but soon after, the weather became overcast with a heavy drizzle. At dusk on the same evening the wind increased to gale force from the south-east with heavy driving rain and a rough sea.

Captain Gilling checked the position of his ship regularly, but at 10.20 p.m., land was sighted close to port beam and the helm was immediately put hard-a-starboard. The ORUNGAL, slow to respond in the conditions, struck rocks at about 10.30 p.m. and stranded approximately three-quarters of a mile east of Barwon Heads on the Formby Reef.

The ship's siren was sounded and rockets fired to raise the alarm in Barwon Heads and the fire bell called together a big group of volunteers.

Mr Clive Stephens attempted to reach the vessel but heavy seas forced him to abandon the attempt, although messages in morse were exchanged and the Queenscliff lifeboat called.

Despite a solid battering throughout the night, the vessel held together well and the passengers and crew were landed safely in Queenscliff after two trips soon after daylight.

Commonwealth salvage experts examined the vessel and decided she could be salvaged but on the morning of December 13th, a few days prior to the first attempt to refloat her, a serious fire broke out on board and several working on her were injured and admitted to hospital. Local fishermen played a major role in their rescue.

The fire damaged the ship beyond repair, and when tenders were called for dismantling, the wrecking firm of Whelan the Wrecker purchased the hulk for £1,175.

They were to spend the next three years cutting it to pieces, and no doubt showed a handsome profit on the sale of miles of copper pipe, winches, fittings, and machinery, some of which was purchased by the American Navy. "We expected her to hold together for about three months, long enough for us to get our money back," Mr Tom Whelan later recalled.

One lifeboat, practically undamaged, was repaired, coated with pitch, nicknamed Black Bess, and used to ferry hundreds of tons of material ashore where it was transported in twelve ton loads on a gas producer powered truck to Melbourne for disposal. Naval experts retrieved the stern gun which was undamaged.

Although visitors were not encouraged, many tourists hired craft to cruise around the wreck, and the hulk was a major tourist attraction for many years.

As the vessel slowly disappeared under the cutting torch the original 11 workmen dwindled to 3, but no decision had been reached regarding her abandonment until one morning, when she was strafed in four runs by an R.A.A.F. fighter aircraft firing live ammunition, sending the three men running for cover.

"We decided that was the finish," Mr Whelan said.

Later the firm advised that it had no further claim on the wreck which reverted back to the Commonwealth.

After the wreckers left, the hulk was gradually battered to pieces, and by 1945 had practically disappeared.

The ship's bell, inscribed FEZARA, her original name, was removed soon after she was wrecked and presented to the owner of the Barwon Heads Hotel.

The Court of Marine Inquiry held at Melbourne exonerated the master of all blame deciding that although the vessel was ten miles off course, this was due to abnormal currents and weather conditions with Captain Gilling unable to verify his position.

It recommended that all coastal ships over a prescribed tonnage be fitted with direction finding apparatus, and also echo sounding equipment to enable the crew to ascertain the depth of water without reducing speed, particularly in view of the extreme danger of delaying outside ports in war time.

ORUNGAL's sister ship, ORMISTON, continued in the coastal trade until 1955 when she was sold to overseas interests.

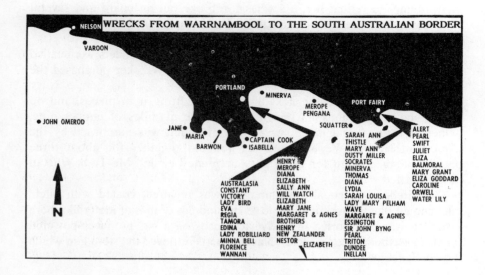

WRECKS FROM WARRNAMBOOL TO THE SOUTH AUSTRALIAN BORDER

4 – Schooners

The schooner rig was the most common used by the early Colonial and coastal traders. The topsail schooner with two or more masts fore and aft rigged also carried square sails on the fore topmast. Fore and aft schooners had two or more masts all fore and aft rigged.

THISTLE – 1837

Built 1750. 64 tons. Bought by the Henty Brothers in 1832. She made several visits to Portland and took Edward Henty there in 1834.

At the conclusion of the 1837 whaling season, the THISTLE was employed carrying bark between Port Fairy and Launceston.

After waiting three days for a wind, she was at anchor off Port Fairy on Christmas Eve, when caught by a strong south-easterly gale. One anchor parted, but she held on the second until mid-afternoon on Christmas Day, when it also went, and she drove ashore close to the old jetty and became a total wreck.

As there was no other vessel in port at the time, Captain Mills and four men sailed on to Port Phillip in a whale boat, arriving safely on January 3rd, 1838.

DUSTY MILLER – 1842

Built 1840. 90 tons. Length 62.8 feet; beam 17.9 feet; depth 9.9 feet.

Bound from Launceston to Portland, she was lost off Port Fairy on November 21st.

When forty miles from her destination, a gale sprang up, forcing Captain Saunders to seek shelter. When she struck the sea swept over her, bringing her on her beam ends, but eventually a line was floated ashore which enabled the passengers and crew with the exception of one passenger, Captain Jenkins, to land safely. Jenkins was washed overboard and drowned.

The vessel and cargo were sold for £45, and most of the cargo was salvaged undamaged.

TRUGANINA – 1842

Built 1839. 61 tons. Length, 56.2 feet; beam, 17.2 feet; depth, 10 feet.

Bound from Portland to Hobart, the TRUGANINA, Captain Griffiths, sheltering in Lady Bay from rough weather, drifted on to rocks on the night of December 2nd, and went to pieces almost immediately.

The crew and passengers reached the shore, but being without food or shelter, Captain Griffiths despatched some of the crew to Melbourne in a small boat to arrange relief. Outside Port Phillip Heads it met the steamer SEA HORSE, which took the seamen on board and towed the boat to Hobson's Bay. Help was immediately sent overland.

ELIZABETH – 1844

A strong south-easterly gale swept Portland Bay on November 18th, destroying two vessels. The schooner ELIZABETH, 58 tons, Captain Tipley, on a voyage from Melbourne to Adelaide, took shelter but was eventually blown ashore and lost.

SALLY ANN – 1844

She was destroyed by the same gale which wrecked the ELIZABETH, and is believed to have been driven on to rocks near the lighthouse. The 52 ton schooner was later sold for £42 and probably dismantled.

SQUATTER – 1846

Built 1845. 50 tons. Length, 53 feet; beam 14.6 feet; depth, 7.9 feet.

Battered by heavy weather after leaving Melbourne for Portland, the SQUATTER ran on to a reef about two miles west of Port Fairy on May 21st, and became a total wreck.

She lay broadside on to the sea and was continually washed by huge breakers, forcing the passengers and crew to tie themselves to the rigging to await some moderation in the weather. It was six hours before they were able to land.

THETIS – 1848

Built 1847. 95 tons. Length, 66.1 feet; beam, 18.4 feet; depth, 9.6 feet.

Inward bound from Sydney, she struck the Point Lonsdale Reef at 9 p.m. on May 26th, with the loss of four lives.

Fifteen minutes after she struck she was on her beam ends with her masts lying over the rocks. The twenty-four passengers, most of whom were in bed at the time, rushed on deck and clung to the side of the vessel. At low tide the passengers and crew were ordered to climb along the masts and down the spars, from which they dropped on to the reef.

Two children were swept from their mother's arms and drowned. Their parents reached the reef in such a distressed and exhausted condition they died before reaching the shore. All other passengers and crew reached safety.

MINERVA – 1849

Built 1847. 83 tons. Length, 60.2 feet; beam, 18.4 feet; depth, 8.7 feet.

On February 6th, she left Sydney for Portland and after being delayed by rough weather, she was off Cape Otway on March 27th, when her master, Captain Hovenden, noticed smoke pouring from the cabin. The vessel carried a large quantity of gunpowder, so it was hurriedly decided to abandon her. Two attempts to return on board were made, but the burning powder ignited the decks causing her masts to fall.

When the MINERVA finally burned down to the water's edge seven hours later, she was about forty miles west of Cape Otway. Captain Hovenden

Does an ancient vessel known as the MAHOGANY SHIP lie buried in the sandhills between Warrnambool and Port Fairy?

H.M.S. SAPPHO, last sighted off Cape Otway in February 1858 during a voyage from England to Sydney.

Remains of the schooner OTWAY on the beach at Lorne. She was lost in 1862.

Anchors from the tea clipper MARIE GABRIELLE, lost on Wreck Beach, 1869.

S.S. EDINA steams out of Lady Bay, Warrnambool in 1867 past the schooners PEVERIL and TOMMY. The remains of the wrecked schooner ENTERPRISE lie in the foreground half buried in the sand.

Tom Pearce
LOCH ARD survivor.

Eva Carmichael
LOCH ARD survivor.

Captain Gibb, master of the LOCH ARD. After his vessel missed stays and both anchors dragged when let go, his desperate efforts to save the ship had almost succeeded when she struck a cliff near Mutton Bird Island.

Sketch from the Australasian Sketcher showing the coastal steamer DAWN rescuing survivors from the wrecked American ship ERIC THE RED near Cape Otway, September 1880.

Smuggling was rife at the wreck of the American ship JOSEPH H. SCAMMELL at Torquay, 1891.

Warrnambool's worst shipping disaster occurred on November 10th 1905 when the New Zealand barquentine LA BELLA struck a reef near the breakwater, drowing seven of her crew of twelve.

*Wine, brandy and sardines were packed aboard the French barque
GLANEUSE when she ran ashore near Point Lonsdale in 1886. Most was
salvaged.*

*The barque EDINBURGH CASTLE loaded with casks of cement for the
Warrnambool breakwater soon went to pieces after going ashore in Lady
Bay, January 1888.*

Crude wooden cross marking the grave of a seaman drowned while salvaging the barque W.B. GODFREY in 1891. Later, when the Great Ocean Road was constructed over the grave a new headstone was erected nearby. (See over page.)

The barque GEORGE ROPER lies totally wrecked at Point Lonsdale, 1883. She was lost during her maiden voyage from Liverpool to Melbourne.

The barque NEWFIELD soon broke up after stranding near Peterborough, 1892. Wreckers and smugglers who hurried to the scene were disappointed to learn she carried salt.

False grave on the cliff at the wreck of the W.B. GODFREY after restoration in 1965.

Fire destroys the American clipper PAUL JONES off Lorne, 1886.

The barque FIJI ashore at Wreck Beach, 1891.

The new iron barque HOLYHEAD lies totally wrecked at Point Lonsdale,
February 12th 1890.

Inward bound to Melbourne from Liverpool, the iron barque INVERLOCHY
lies totally wrecked near Anglesea, December 1902.

The big four masted barque FALLS OF HALLADALE grounded on a reef west of Peterborough 1908.

SPECULANT

WRECKED CAPE PATTEN 10/2/11

After rounding Cape Otway in a gale on her way from Portland to Melbourne, the barquentine SPECULANT was forced ashore on Cape Patten by a gale and lost, February 1911.

Survivors from the WOLLOMAI, wrecked near Apollo Bay, June 1923.

S.S. CASINO, the most famous steamer in the West Coast Trade until lost at Apollo Bay on July 10th 1932.

The American steamer CITY OF RAYVILLE became the first United States vessel lost in World War 2 when mined off Cape Otway on November 8th 1940.

S.S. ORUNGAL destroyed by fire as she lies stranded off Barwon Heads, December 1940.

WRECK OF THE **LOCH ARD**

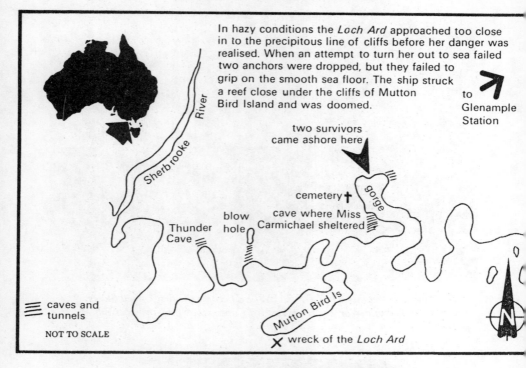

In hazy conditions the *Loch Ard* approached too close in to the precipitous line of cliffs before her danger was realised. When an attempt to turn her out to sea failed two anchors were dropped, but they failed to grip on the smooth sea floor. The ship struck a reef close under the cliffs of Mutton Bird Island and was doomed.

to Glenample Station

Sherbrooke River

two survivors came ashore here

cemetery †

cave where Miss Carmichael sheltered

gorge

Thunder Cave

blow hole

Mutton Bird Is

✕ wreck of the *Loch Ard*

≡ caves and tunnels

NOT TO SCALE

N

FINAL MOMENTS OF SS **CASINO**

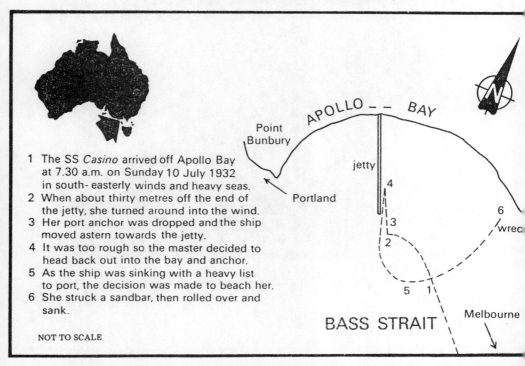

1 The SS *Casino* arrived off Apollo Bay at 7.30 a.m. on Sunday 10 July 1932 in south-easterly winds and heavy seas.
2 When about thirty metres off the end of the jetty, she turned around into the wind.
3 Her port anchor was dropped and the ship moved astern towards the jetty.
4 It was too rough so the master decided to head back out into the bay and anchor.
5 As the ship was sinking with a heavy list to port, the decision was made to beach her.
6 She struck a sandbar, then rolled over and sank.

NOT TO SCALE

APOLLO - - BAY

Point Bunbury

jetty

Portland

4

3

2

6

wrec

5   1

BASS STRAIT

Melbourne

N

decided to sail for Port Fairy, but adverse winds forced him to eventually set a course for Port Phillip. For four days they ran before heavy squalls and rough seas, before landing near The Heads where they met up with Pilots McPherson and Timothy.

DAVID – 1850

The schooner DAVID, 80 tons, Captain Hills, left Hobart for Melbourne with four passengers and a cargo of timber, but struck the Point Lonsdale Reef at midnight on April 14th, and commenced to bump heavily.

At low water the reef was quite dry and the vessel was found to be lying in a hollow formed to her shape by the continued pounding on the soft rock. Early the following morning, she began to take water rapidly, so all hands took to the boats, into which the mails and ship's papers were also placed. The DAVID filled and partially broke up with the next tide and during the night completely disappeared.

ENTERPRISE – 1850

Built 1847. 58 tons. Length, 49 feet; beam, 16.6 feet; depth, 9 feet.

She was anchored in Lady Bay, Warrnambool, on September 14th, prior to sailing with a full cargo of potatoes and wheat when a gale forced her ashore.

The wind commenced from the south and gradually veered to the south-east, increasing to gale force. She carried only one anchor and when this dragged, she lost her rudder and blew broadside on the surf well up on the sand. An Aboriginal named Buckawall swam out with a rope tied around his waist, and despite a terrific buffeting succeeded in getting a line aboard, enabling Captain Caught and his crew to land. One man was suffering from exposure and exhaustion, but later recovered. Efforts to salvage her failed and she was eventually sold. A memorial plaque to the ENTERPRISE may be seen today at St John's Presbyterian Church, Warrnambool.

CAPTAIN COOK – 1850

Built 1847. 74 tons. Length, 62.2 feet; beam, 17.4 feet; depth, 10 feet.

When the schooner CAPTAIN COOK, bound from Mersey River, Tasmania, to Adelaide, was off Moonlight Head, she was struck by a terrific gale which blew her between the Lawrence Rocks and Cape Nelson.

Her master, Captain Roberts, worked desperately to sail out of this dangerous position, but eventually the schooner was driven on to the rocks in the bight formed by Capes Grant and Nelson, where she became a total wreck.

The passengers and crew reached safety but the mails were lost. The wreck and cargo were sold on the beach fifteen days later for £83/12/6.

MARY JANE – 1852

A gale destroyed the schooner MARY JANE, 81 tons, at Portland on May 1st.

ELIZABETH – 1852

The schooner ELIZABETH, 80 tons, Captain Wyse, left Williamstown on May 12th for Adelaide, but when off Cape Otway she sprang a leak. The pumps were manned, but when they became blocked with sand being carried as ballast, she became unmanageable and eventually ran ashore on May 14th at a point now unknown. As she lay broadside on to the beach, the passengers and crew landed and erected sails for shelter before returning for provisions and a supply of spirits. Parties set out to seek an overland route to Geelong, but after encountering steep ranges and thick bush, returned to the wreck. Another party of twelve set out for Geelong several days later, but the remainder were rescued by the COLINA and landed at Sandridge.

As a token of their gratitude the rescued party presented the COLINA's captain with a gold watch and chain and a sum of money to be divided among his crew. (This vessel may have been refloated.)

LILLIAS – 1852

The 89 ton vessel, built in Tasmania in 1839 and commanded by Captain Hannah, attempted to beat out of Lady Bay, Warrnambool, during a south-westerly gale on December 29th, but ran ashore near the Hopkins River.

Although an enormous sea was running, those on shore believed her safe, but as she passed the eastern reef a lull in the wind caused her to lose way and she ran ashore, becoming a total wreck.

FREEDOM – 1853

A schooner of 165 tons, she was anchored in Warrnambool harbour on July 11th, with a cargo of wheat and flour for Sydney, when she parted her chains during a gale and drifted ashore near the jetty. Her master, Captain Noon, who was ashore attending to private business, hurried to the beach, but little could be done until the sea moderated.

She was refloated soon after with some of her cargo still aboard, but on October 11th, she was again driven ashore where she became a total wreck, her hull being sold by auction on the beach for £268.

OSPREY – 1854

Built 1834. 149 tons. Length, 78.8 feet; beam, 20.7 feet; depth, 13.7 feet.

This three-masted schooner in charge of Captain Hawkins, went ashore near the mouth of the Erskine River with two anchors down early on Sunday, June 18th.

Although the wind was gale force and huge waves were breaking over her, all hands and most of her gear were saved.

When the storm abated she was left lying on her side, only a few yards out, but badly sanded up. Her owners believed she could be salvaged, but their attempts failed and she became a total wreck.

REBEL – 1855

Built 1833. 104 tons. Length, 71.8 feet; beam, 17.9 feet; depth, 11.9 feet.
The REBEL, registered at Geelong was wrecked in Loutit Bay on February 17th, during a south-easterly gale. Portion of the vessel and a few stores were salvaged.

SWIFT – 1855

The three-masted schooner SWIFT, 120 tons, bound from Launceston to Port Fairy, with a cargo of timber, was lost on Griffiths Island on June 19. The weather was hazy and the schooner struck a reef on the south side of the island, becoming a total wreck. No lives were lost, although one man was struck by a falling mast.

ANNIE – 1857

She struck at Haley Reef near Apollo Bay during a gale on November 30th, but her crew remained on board, hoping that she might be refloated. However, after several days, she began to break up and the crew were forced to abandon her. The ANNIE was a vessel of 103 tons.

NONPAREIL – 1857

The NONPAREIL, 186 tons, Captain Creswell, on a voyage from Adelaide to Melbourne with a cargo of flour, was wrecked on the Point Lonsdale Reef on the night of October 13th.
She was discovered next morning by the outside pilot vessel and the Queens-cliff lifeboat was immediately despatched to her aid, rescuing fifteen passengers and five members of the crew. However, the captain and three crewmen who left the ship in a boat to seek aid soon after she struck were not seen again.

MARTHA – 1858

Built 1847. 109 tons. Length, 69.5 feet; beam, 17.8 feet; depth, 11.9 feet.
Late in February she was unloading timber at the mouth of the Parker River for extensions at the Cape Otway lighthouse when an easterly gale broke without warning. She attempted to beat out to sea, but was driven ashore on the eastern side of Point Franklin. The crew landed safely and made their way overland to Geelong.

TOROA – 1858

The TOROA, 58 tons, left Warrnambool for Melbourne on August 6th with twelve passengers and a full cargo but failed to arrive. Part of her cargo, a case of toys, washed up at Barwon Heads, indicated that she had probably foundered after rounding Cape Otway.

ANONYMA – 1859

Built 1847. 75 tons. Length, 62.1 feet; beam, 19.2 feet; depth, 7.5 feet.
A pilot schooner, she had been cruising off The Heads throughout Sunday, October 2nd, and as a northerly gale was blowing she kept close inshore.

During the night, the wind swung to the south, forcing her on to a lee shore. The gale was so strong she was unable to carry sufficient canvas to beat to windward and she struck the Lonsdale Reef. The crew took to the boat, but when it capsized they were forced to swim to shore.

ELIZABETH – 1860

Built 1848. 90 tons. Length, 66.3 feet; beam, 17.1 feet; depth, 9.5 feet.
Bound from Port Fairy to Melbourne, she struck Point Lonsdale Reef on the night of April 22nd, during a heavy squall. No lives were lost, but on the following day, the masts went overboard, then she quickly went to pieces.

PRINCE OF WALES – 1861

At daylight on January 7th, the schooner PRINCE OF WALES, 112 tons, commanded by Captain Campbell, was seen to be on the Lonsdale Reef and shortly afterwards, two of her boats arrived at Queenscliff. Her captain reported she was from Circular Head, Tasmania, with fifteen passengers and a cargo of timber, and she had run on to the reef on the previous evening, while standing off and waiting for first light, to go through The Rip.

Although the Customs and Health Officers' boats with the pilot schooners RIP and PROSPERINE, also the tug SOPHIA, were promptly alongside, they could save little and the schooner soon became a total wreck.

ELIZA – 1866

The schooner ELIZA, 94 tons, Captain Stobaus, laden with timber from Corner Inlet, entered Port Fairy Bay and anchored at the Government moorings in strong winds and choppy seas. The wind increased and the schooner began to drag, breaking her moorings and driving ashore opposite the botanical gardens. The crew took to the rigging to escape the seas, which were sweeping over the wreck but Captain Mills and a crew launched a boat, and eventually took them off. The rocket crew also stood by on the beach.

LADY ROBILLIARD – 1867

One of the worst gales ever recorded in Portland's early history burst over the port on September 22nd.

Two vessels, the LADY ROBILLIARD and PHILIPPINE were anchored in the bay, but by evening on the second day, only the PHILIPPINE remained.

Giant waves broke five miles off shore and at times were running over the foreyards of the vessels, as they pitched and rolled in an alarming manner. A tremendous sea struck the 52 ton LADY ROBILLIARD and this was followed by another which caused her anchor chain to part. The second anchor was let go, but the force of the wind caused her to drag until it also parted, and she drifted helplessly ashore near Whaler's Bluff.

Throughout the night nothing could be done to rescue the crew, but next morning a cable was fastened to the vessel and the crew brought ashore.

MARY CUMMINGS – 1872

Built 1861. 106 tons. Length, 81.3 feet; beam, 21.1 feet; depth, 10.3 feet.

The schooner MARY CUMMINGS, left Melbourne for Port McDonnell in ballast but soon after passing Point Lonsdale ran into fog and heavy seas. Her master, Captain Wigmore, estimated the vessel to be at least 10 miles off shore when she ran into the breakers in the early morning of November 23rd.

With the heavy seas which break off Cape Patten rolling over her, two anchors were let out to hold her shortly before the crew of six took to the boat which was provisioned with gin and biscuits.

The crew rowed the boat east for 30 hours in travelling 40 miles to Barwon Heads, where they landed, narrowly escaping being capsized in the surf, although their biscuits were spoilt by salt water. From Barwon Heads, the crew walked overland to Point Lonsdale lighthouse, and the news was telegraphed to Melbourne.

The tug MYSTERY took on extra cable and seven hands before setting out through the fog to Cape Patten. When the tug arrived the vessel was still holding on the edge of the breakers, but while preparations were being made to take her in tow, a large roller tore away one anchor and she drove ashore.

A Court of Inquiry found that an error in the compass was responsible for the loss of the vessel and her master was exonerated from blame.

DON – 1875

Built 1864. 57 tons. Length, 72.2 feet; beam, 17.4 feet; depth, 7.2 feet.

The schooner DON, outward bound from Melbourne to Tasmania in ballast, drifted on to the Point Lonsdale Reef during a calm on July 2nd.

As the vessel drifted close to the reef, a boat was lowered and a kedge anchor used in an attempt to haul the vessel away, but an outlying rock caught her on the starboard bow, and canted her on to the reef. The set of the tide then hove her upon a flat portion of the reef where she remained.

The crew were landed by the Queenscliff lifeboat and all moveable gear was landed before the vessel broke up a few days later.

WATER LILY – 1876

The schooner WATER LILY, 51 tons, Captain McDougall, bound from Port McDonnell to Port Pirie, drifted ashore on the south-west point of Griffiths Island, Port Fairy, on June 26th. The vessel had lost her rudder and sprung a leak during heavy weather soon after sailing, and, having become unmanageable, she was abandoned. She then apparently drifted along the coast until she struck the island.

At the Marine Board Inquiry, Captain McDougall admitted that the schooner had five feet of water in the hold when she sailed.

This was the last major wreck at Port Fairy.

YOUNG AUSTRALIA – 1877

The three-masted schooner YOUNG AUSTRALIA, 130 tons, under the command of Captain W. Whitfield, bound from Maryborough, Queensland, for Adelaide with a cargo of 70 hogsheads and some quarter-casks of rum, also about 150 tons of sugar, went ashore at Curdie's Inlet on May 25th.

When off Cape Nelson, she was caught in rough weather which carried away her rigging, causing the fore top mast to fall, springing the foremast.

Captain Whitfield endeavoured to sail for Portland, but the vessel proved almost unmanageable, and after being on the verge of foundering stern first, struggled to a point east of Curdie's Inlet where anchors were dropped.

A tremendous sea soon drove her ashore onto a sandbar near the mouth of the river, where she was holed and battered by a succession of enormous waves, which kept her crew of six under shelter.

Finally, one of the crew endeavoured to reach the shore with a line, but he was drowned when it became saturated and sagged into the surf. Those remaining waited on the vessel for about four more hours before a line was floated ashore and fastened to a horse and dray which kept it taut until all had reached safety.

The vessel was insured for £2,000 and her cargo for £5,000, but local interests were able to purchase her for £480. They salvaged a considerable amount of cargo, although most of the sugar was badly damaged.

A Court of Inquiry found that defective equipment caused her loss, but the master retained his certificate.

BLACK WITCH I – 1954

Built 1914. 55 tons. Originally steel screw steamer CHEOPIS. Length, 70 feet; beam, 14 feet; depth, 9 feet.

BLACK WITCH II – 1958

Built 1924. 60 tons. Originally H.M.A.S. CERBERUS. Length, 70 feet; beam, 14 feet.

Jim Anderson of Apollo Bay, who loved ships in the fine old tradition of sail, purchased these two vessels, converted them to his own plans, but unfortunately lost both in his home port during violent easterlies.

BLACK WITCH I, first used by the Customs at Adelaide and then employed in the passenger trade to Kangaroo Island, was a well-appointed little vessel when Anderson purchased her for his fishing enterprises.

On the night of January 22nd, 1954, during an easterly gale, she was washed ashore and badly holed. Several attempts to refloat her failed and she was finally abandoned.

Her successor had been fishing in Tasmanian waters, when Anderson returned to Apollo Bay to visit his father, who was very ill in hospital.

Caught in yet another easterly, she dragged into the surf and was lost, the three men narrowly escaping with their lives.

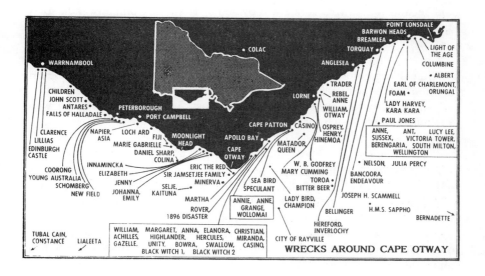

WRECKS AROUND CAPE OTWAY

DIVERS, SHIPWRECKS ON THE VICTORIAN
WEST COAST ARE PROTECTED
UNDER COMMONWEALTH AND STATE
HISTORIC SHIPWRECKS LEGISLATION

5 – Brigs & Brigantines

Brigs are two-masted sailing vessels with square sails on each mast, also fore and aft sails.
Brigantines also have two masts, the foremast being square rigged and the main mast fore and aft rigged.

DIANA – 1844

The brig DIANA, 103 tons, went ashore at Port Fairy on October 1st, and became a total wreck. She was owned by Henty & Company and carried a cargo from Sydney. The wreck was eventually sold to Mr Griffiths for £13.

ELIZABETH – 1846

After riding out a south-easterly gale for two days, the brig ELIZABETH, 230 tons, laden with whale oil and wool broke her moorings and went ashore at Portland on November 26th and was lost. The vessel and cargo were auctioned on the beach for £240.

SARAH LOUISA – 1849

Captain Charles Mills, later Harbour Master at Port Fairy, was in charge of this brig, a vessel of 216 tons, when she was lost at Port Fairy on July 6th.

She arrived from Melbourne and was loading a cargo for Sydney when a storm sprang up. She dragged two anchors until her port chain broke and she went ashore. A few minutes after she struck, the Second Mate was washed overboard but was rescued by a man who braved the rough seas and hauled him ashore. A seaman who went to the Mate's assistance was swept out to sea but a boat put off and rescued him also. Soon after midday the foremast went over the side, pitching three men who were clinging to it into the sea. They were saved as were the mate and two seamen who remained on the main top, but the steward and cook who took refuge on deck were drowned.

LADY MARY PELHAM – 1849

A gale drove the brig ashore on the morning of August 31st, while she was waiting for a fair wind to help her on a voyage to Sydney.

The vessel of 184 tons, owned by S.G. Henty, master Captain Wing, had parted her anchors and was drifting shorewards when her master set all possible sail and ran her high on to the beach. The shock broke her wheel and sent the crew sprawling over the deck, but everyone reached safety. Later, she broke her back and became a total wreck.

ESSINGTON - 1852

Springing a leak while anchored at Port Fairy, this brig of 123 tons was beached near the mouth of the Moyne River and eventually became a total wreck.

MARGARET & AGNES - 1852

A brigantine of 103 tons, she went ashore at Portland on May 23rd and became a total wreck.

SIR JOHN BYNG - 1852

The brig, SIR JOHN BYNG, 177 tons, Captain Frith, was lost at Port Fairy during the same gale. She carried a small cannon which her master had purchased in Sydney from H.M. Brig FANTOME, which had been dismantled in 1841. Thirteen years later high tides exposed the wreck and the cannon was located and put on display at the Port Fairy Mechanics' Institute. The hull was eventually broken up and burned to recover copper bolts and metal sheathing.

JENNY - 1854

Everyone loves a sea mystery, and for several generations the old rusted swivel headed anchor, wedged in a cleft a few feet above high water on an almost inaccessible section of coast a short distance east of Moonlight Head has puzzled the few who have stumbled over it during fishing or exploratory expeditions.

Although it was lying on the rocks when the area was first settled, its location and size indicate that it probably came from the brig JENNY, lost in 1854.

A vessel of 224 tons, bound from Bristol to Melbourne, she drifted ashore during a calm in February and became a total wreck.

The Government brig, PACIFICO, rescued the master, Captain J. Liciss, the crew and the one passenger, transporting them to Melbourne.

COLUMBINE - 1854

The COLUMBINE, a brig of 180 tons, built at Aberdeen in 1839, and inward bound from Liverpool to Geelong with a general cargo was wrecked off Ocean Grove on April 1st with a loss of four lives.

The pilot, Matthew Davidson, boarded the vessel in fine, clear weather but soon after, the master, Captain McLennan, uneasy about his course, attempted to interfere, with negative results.

At 10 p.m., the vessel ran on to a shoal off Ocean Grove which runs eastward for about a mile and after striking about five times the tiller and rudder broke allowing the sea to enter. At 3 a.m. the following morning all hands left the ship and pulled for the shore.

The gig reached the shore safely but the long boat carrying the captain, his brother, sister, and twelve others capsized in the surf drowning the pilot, the captain's sister, and Mr and Mrs Clarke.

At daylight, the wreck was seen from Point Lonsdale by the pilot schooner BOOM-ERANG, and lifeboats were sent. Pilot Davidson left a wife and six children.

ELANORA – 1856

On December 30th, the ELANORA, 180 tons, registered at Melbourne was anchored off Apollo Bay loading sleepers for the Geelong to Ballarat railway when a strong easterly gale sprang up and washed her ashore where she became a wreck in less than an hour.

LADY HARVEY – 1858

The LADY HARVEY of 146 tons, inward bound from Tasmania with a cargo of timber for the Williamstown jetty, ran on the rocks off the bluff at Barwon Heads during a gale on the 14th of February and became a total wreck.

Captain Curtis and the crew swam ashore but, unfortunately, one man was swept away and drowned. Mr McDonald, a local settler, gave them unlimited assistance before they proceeded to Geelong.

Four years earlier, on April 29th, 1854, inward bound from Glasgow, she had run ashore at Point Lonsdale a few miles to the east, but was towed clear by the tug LIONESS.

JOHN SCOTT – 1858

Soon after the brig JOHN SCOTT of 157 tons gross left Adelaide on January 27th, she ran into thick fog and heavy weather causing her master, Captain R. Gunn, a great deal of anxiety as he endeavoured to ascertain the vessel's position en route to Melbourne.

At about 1 a.m. on the morning of February 14th, she struck a reef near Flaxman's Hill, 15 miles east of Warrnambool.

The five passengers and crew remained on the ship until daylight when Captain Gunn sounded the holds and found them full of water.

Plans were immediately prepared for the landing of the passengers comprising Mr and Mrs Gursen, their two children, and Mr Alfred. Immediately they reached the shore all were taken to the nearby McReddin station, where they were given dry clothing.

The wreck was later sold for £250 and much of the cargo comprising 1,000 bushels of wheat, 9,000 bushels of bran, 59 tons of flour, 4 tons of smeltered copper was recovered although most of the grain was badly damaged by water.

MAID OF JULPHA – 1859

A vessel of 300 tons burthen, she arrived in Lady Bay, Warrnambool from Singapore on January 15th with a cargo of tea, sugar, spices, tobacco, ale, spirits and fancy goods.

At about 4.30 a.m. next morning the crew of the PEVERIL, anchored nearby, noticed her cookhouse on fire and raised the alarm. Captain Beauvais and his crew cut holes in the deck in an attempt to reach the fire, but it gradually increased, finally driving them to the boats.

At about 5 a.m. an attempt was made to beach her, but the intense heat prevented the harbour master and his crew remaining nearby for very long while cutting the cable. Eventually they succeeded and despite a heavy surge, beached her about three hours before both masts fell and she burned to the waterline.

Most of the loss was the captain's, although the cargo, valued at £4,000 was insured for £2,000. The vessel, which had only recently been copper sheathed, rigged and renovated was valued at £2,800. The captain's wife and the crew saved only a few articles of clothing, and although Customs men kept a careful watch on portion of the cargo, after it floated ashore, some was stolen.

HERCULES – 1861

Laden with timber this 140 ton brigantine was driven ashore at Apollo Bay during a gale on December 15th. Her master had secured three anchors and believed her safe, but the strong current and heavy ground swell threw her high onto the beach. No lives were lost.

JULIA – 1863

Disaster struck the occupants of a whale boat which left the whaling station at Portland to rescue the crew of the wrecked brig JULIA.

The JULIA, a vessel of 111 tons, was travelling in ballast from Adelaide to Melbourne when damaged by a gale off Cape Jaffa and forced ashore on the Narrawong coast on August 2nd.

A report was relayed to Portland and the lifeboat succeeded in rescuing Captain Dart and his crew shortly before the vessel drifted ashore.

Unfortunately, the whale boat capsized in heavy seas drowning the six occupants. Only three bodies were recovered.

GOLDEN SPRING – 1863

The GOLDEN SPRING called into Warrnambool in July, during a voyage from Melbourne to Adelaide to load 90 tons of potatoes.

Early on the morning of July 6th, a gale sprang up and at about 9 a.m. she dragged her anchors into the surf, appearing to strike the wreck of the MAID OF JULPHA about 150 yards out.

The first line, floated ashore on a cask, broke, but soon after a second line was attached. Captain Kelly and eight members of the crew reached safety. The brig, 170 tons, American built and Sydney owned, broke in two before noon and became a total wreck.

FAIR TASMANIAN – 1864

Built 1850. 200 tons burden.

Late in the evening of May 27th, while preparing to leave Lady Bay, Warrnambool, with 185 tons of potatoes, the FAIR TASMANIAN began to pitch in a rising sea until, without warning, one of her anchor chains parted causing her to swing alarmingly on her second anchor. Her master, Captain Francis, was not unduly alarmed, stationing a member of the crew forward in case of emergency. However, when her second anchor parted, sail was set in an attempt to beach her head on. Dragging anchor chains made her difficult to manage and she drifted ashore near where the PEVERIL had been stranded a year earlier.

Guns were fired and bells rung to attract attention ashore where the rocket crew was soon assembled to proceed to the wreck. Four rockets were fired before a line was attached enabling the crew to struggle ashore, leaving the captain's wife and four-year-old daughter to be brought ashore in a boat. Unfortunately it was swamped in the surf tossing the occupants into the sea, where after some anxious moments the girl was swept ashore to safety, while the remainder regained the ship.

At their second attempt, this time along the line, Mrs Francis caught her hair in the running block and her life was endangered until portion of her hair was cut away.

Next day, when the seas abated, the crew returned to salvage spars, rigging and personal effects. The hull was eventually purchased for £31, the cargo, spoiled by the sea brought a mere £1, while the sails and spars made £16-9-0. The cargo was insured for £500.

BALMORAL – 1868

A heavy south-easterly gale drove the brigantine BALMORAL ashore on July 9th while she was loading potatoes for Adelaide. Immediately she struck, the 106 ton vessel went to pieces.

YARROW – 1870

Built 1851. 229 tons. Length, 99 feet; beam, 20.5 feet; depth, 14.5 feet.

The crew of nine on the brig YARROW dropped into the sea from the vessel's yards and were rescued by the Queenscliff lifeboat and S.S. MYSTERY, after she struck the Point Lonsdale Reef on August 23rd while entering Port Phillip Heads with a cargo of coal from Newcastle.

ALEXANDRA – 1882

The brig, ALEXANDRA, 239 tons, Captain Jones, loaded with 130 tons of potatoes, was lying at anchor in Lady Bay when a heavy gale struck early in the morning of March 30th.

At about 1 a.m. both her cables parted and she ran stern on to the beach east of the jetties. The Mate struggled to shore with a line, and later several of the crew reached the beach, although the cook was almost drowned. The vessel commenced to break up next day.

YARRA – 1882

Built 1850. 141 tons. Length, 88.3 feet; beam, 21.7 feet; depth, 10 feet.

The brigantine YARRA, Captain Shealer, arrived from Newcastle with 193 tons of coal early in October and was anchored in Lady Bay when a heavy swell caused her anchors to part. She drifted across the bay out of control, first colliding with S.S. DAWN before grounding east of the jetties with her masts and bowsprit badly damaged.

She broke up next day and became a total wreck. The DAWN suffered only superficial damage.

JANE - 1882

Yet another vessel was lost at Warrnambool when the brigantine JANE, loaded with coal from Newcastle, was wrecked west of the jetty on October 21st. There was no loss of life, but the captain and crew lost all their possessions.

WOLLOMAI - 1923

Built 1876. 143 tons. Length, 107.6 feet; beam, 23.6 feet; depth, 9.5 feet.

At about 8 p.m. on the night of June 4th, distress signals were observed at Mounts Bay, near the Henty Reef, about two miles south of Apollo Bay. The rocket crew led by Constable Haywood set out for the beach but, owing to the Barrum River bridges washing away, a five-mile detour was necessary. At times the crew struggled through water up to their waists, but eventually the wreck was reached at about 1 a.m. in the morning.

The WOLLOMAI, fully loaded with palings, posts, apples and kerosene was sailing from Burnie to Adelaide, but a strong south-westerly gale had made her unmanageable and she had driven ashore. The vessel was about 50 yards out and mountainous seas were breaking over her.

The rocket crew secured a line almost immediately and Captain O'Neill, a woman passenger and the crew of nine brought safely ashore. The last man left the wreck at 3 a.m.

Heavy seas battered the vessel for days, and she soon moved closer inshore becoming firmly embedded in the sand.

A syndicate of local men purchased the wreck and its cargo, salvaging large quantities of palings and sections of the vessel.

A preliminary inquiry was held at Melbourne, when the master and crew were passing through on their way home to Adelaide. From the evidence presented the board formed the opinion that Captain O'Neill had done everything possible under the circumstances, and no further action was taken to hold a formal investigation.

6 – The Mosquito Fleet

Vessels of 50 tons or less.

Small craft played a prominent role in the development of trade around the West Coast from about 1840 until World War I.

Portland, Port Fairy and Warrnambool used them exclusively until a regular steamship service came into operation in the 1850s, but the ports of Apollo Bay and Lorne continued to use them to send their sleepers, split posts, barrel staves and dairy produce to Melbourne and Geelong.

The coastline between Portland and Point Lonsdale had no anchorages considered safe in all weathers, while Port Campbell, entered through a channel between two reefs, was considered only suitable for small craft with local knowledge.

Many small vessels were stranded or wrecked when caught at anchor after a gale sprang up without warning, or after battling unfavourable winds and seas for days, sometimes even weeks.

DATE UNKNOWN

The schooner TAM O'SHANTER was lost in Portland Bay.

1836

The Warrnambool historian, William Osburne, recorded that the cutter SARAH ANN, 46 tons, was wrecked at Port Fairy on January 14th.

1839

Some old records show that the schooner MARIA was lost near Portland but no information is available.

In the same year, the cutter MEROPE was lost at Portland. She left for Adelaide in February and apparently struck a reef near Lawrence Rocks. All the crew and passengers reached the shore.

1840

The small barque MARY was reported lost in Portland Bay.

1841

The cutter ISABELLA ran ashore and was lost near Point Lonsdale on January 9th, all passengers and crew being rescued and taken on to Melbourne aboard the cutter SISTERS.

1843

The cutter THOMAS, 20 tons, drifted ashore at Port Fairy and became a total wreck.

The schooner JOANNA, under the command of Captain Irving sailed from Launceston for Portland on September 13th, and several days later after battling south-westerly gales was wrecked at the mouth of a small river, a few miles west of Cape Otway. One member of the crew was washed overboard and drowned when she struck, but the captain and crew waded ashore at low tide and reached civilization after eight days of hardship.

Soon after the wreck was abandoned, Aborigines forced the hatches and stole most of the cargo which included spirits and wine, but this did not deter Captain Irving chartering the cutter BARBARA and attempting to return to the wreck to salvage cargo. Adverse weather forced him to abandon these plans, but he did travel overland to her to find most of value gone.

Then, Captain Mills, the well-known Port Fairy whaler engaged four men to carry out salvage, but when attempting a landing nearby, their small boat capsized and two were drowned. Those surviving subsequently took ten days to reach Allen's station on the Hopkins River, eventually returning to Port Fairy with a glowing account of the valuable cargo, high and dry on the beach. Fifteen men returned to the wreck, but little of value remained.

The JOANNA, a schooner of 22 tons, was owned by J. Jellie of Port Fairy, who had it named after his wife.

1853

The schooner HENRY, 48 tons, a well-known trader between Melbourne and the west coast ports, went ashore at Portland in September and was lost.

1857

While loading timber at Portland the schooner VICTORY was blown ashore and lost.

1862

The schooner OTWAY, 33 tons, registered at Geelong, was lost at Lorne. Heavy seas and gale force winds battered her, finally forcing her ashore, where she became a total wreck.

1863

Less than a year later the schooner ANNE, 35 tons, was lost nearby.

1867

On April 17th, S.S. COORONG, on her passage from Adelaide to Melbourne, picked up a boat 25 miles west of Cape Otway containing Captain Stewart and the crew of the schooner BLACK WATCH, which they had abandoned the night before.

The BLACK WATCH, sailed from Warrnambool to Adelaide with a cargo of potatoes and was returning to Melbourne when the leak was discovered. Despite desperate efforts the water gained, and when the cabin floor was covered to a depth of more than a foot, she was abandoned. At daylight she had disappeared.

1868

The ketch PHOENIX, 24 tons, employed salvaging cargo from the wrecked LIGHT OF THE AGE was stranded nearby on March 13th. She was refloated, then burnt at Western Port, 1876.

The cutter LUCY LEE, 14 tons, Captain Webb, bound from Melbourne to Apollo Bay, met heavy weather after clearing Port Phillip Heads on October 29th, and when her sails, anchors and chains proved inadequate, she drifted ashore near Bream Creek.

Soon after she struck, a passenger, Robert Lacey was knocked overboard by the main boom and drowned, but the others reached safety.

A Board of Inquiry later determined that Lacey was knocked overboard by the boom during the reefing of the mainsail, but the conditions prevented efforts being made to rescue him. The vessel carried defective sails, anchors and chains. When the vessel drifted towards shore, anchors were let go, but the chains parted. Captain Webb's certificate was cancelled for twelve months.

1878

The ketch HENRY, 32 tons, visited Lorne regularly with provisions, building materials and general supplies, over a period of many years prior to the construction of the track from Winchelsea, across the Otways to the coast.

The only landing point was a small jetty near the mouth of the Erskine River, and it was found more convenient to beach the vessel on a rising tide, using kedge anchors to haul it onto the beach. After unloading, timber, wattle bark, or ballast was taken on board and she was floated off on a falling tide.

During the HENRY's visit in August, a strong wind drove her hard ashore. Efforts to refloat her failed and soon after, rising wind and sea from the east battered her to pieces.

1881

The schooner MIRANDA, 40 tons, with a full cargo including 600 bags of potatoes grown by the Cawood family, was blown ashore at Apollo Bay below the site of the present golf house, on August 16th. Prior to her stranding, she had been engaged collecting wreckage from ERIC THE RED, and trading between Lorne and Apollo Bay.

1882

The ketch SWAN left Apollo Bay on October 28th for Melbourne, but sprang a leak. She returned next morning and was beached near the jetty, where bad weather destroyed her.

1883

The cutter ALEXANDER, 18 tons, drove ashore at Apollo Bay during an easterly and broke up in the early hours of November 3rd. She was partly loaded with potatoes, all of which were lost.

1888

Members of the Hampshire family arrived off the mouth of the Joanna in the ketch EMILY, 16 tons, Captain Forbes, but owing to mountainous seas was forced to stand off. Later, a boat conveying them ashore was swamped in the surf, but a human chain, organized by lighthouse man, Mr Garner, soon rescued them. The EMILY's single anchor cable later parted in the heavy seas, and she was driven ashore and wrecked.

1889

The topsail schooner TRADER, 45 tons, after a colourful career which included strandings at Warrnambool and St. Leonards was wrecked four miles east of Lorne on the evening of April 2nd.

All hands, consisting of three seamen and Captain Stanton were saved. The schooner, which carried a cargo for Gabo Island, was jammed between two rocks and broke up the following day.

1890

The ketch ALBERT, 42 tons, left Lorne on the morning of August 13th to sail to Melbourne, but sprang a leak in rough seas. Her call for assistance was answered by the pilot schooner RIP, which took her in tow until she foundered about three miles outside The Heads.

The hull was eventually anchored close in shore near Cape Schanck, but when a party arrived to blow it up, it had disappeared.

1894

The ketch W.J. TAYLOR, 44 tons, Captain McLeod, inward bound from Western Port with eight passengers and a crew of three went ashore on Point Lonsdale at 3 a.m. on December 26th. No lives were lost, but the ketch broke up next day.

1895

The schooner SEABIRD, 13 tons, owned by her master, Captain Jeffery and Mr Costin, hotelkeeper of Apollo Bay, was wrecked near Cape Patten on March 6th.

She had arrived from Melbourne with a general cargo and left Apollo Bay the same evening with a load of split posts for Portarlington, and butter and cheese for Melbourne.

Although there was a strong south-westerly and rough seas, Captain Jeffery, who had traded with the port for some years, was not concerned. However, the schooner drove ashore soon after leaving Apollo Bay. Jeffery and one crew member reached safety. The SEABIRD was not insured.

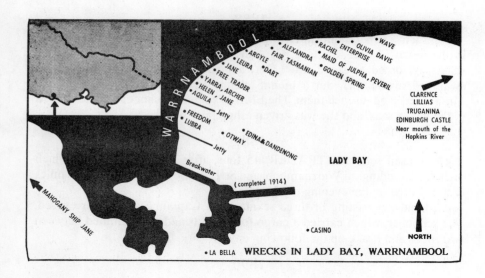

WRECKS IN LADY BAY, WARRNAMBOOL

7 – The Mahogany Ship and Other Mysteries

"Well to the eastward of Gorman's Lane. Proceed eastward till you bring the point of land on which the iron church stood, in line with the highest points of Tower Hill Island. The wreck would be almost in straight line with those objects, well in the hummocks."

This description, given by Captain Mills of Port Fairy in 1836, provides us with the first authentic bearing on an ancient vessel believed buried on the beach, west of Warrnambool, known as the MAHOGANY SHIP.

The wreck was first seen by white men in 1836 when three men, Gibb, Wilson and Smith pursued a seal into Lady Bay. When attempting to enter the Hopkins River, their whaleboat was upset in the surf. Smith was drowned, but the two survivors struggled ashore and set out to return to Belfast, now Port Fairy, on foot, by way of the beach.

Near Tower Hill they came across the remains of an ancient wreck, half buried in the sand, and reported their discovery to Captain John Mills and his brother Charles, both of Belfast.

Although it seems to have been a subject of great interest to district residents, and was visited on many occasions, very little was done to discover its identity during the fifty or so years it lay uncovered. Then, while all visitors to the wreck agreed it lay a considerable distance from the sea, estimates on this point showed a great variation. Osburne, an early Warrnambool historian, claimed it lay "three or four hundred yards off the ocean". Captain Mason of Belfast described it as, "embedded in the sand high and dry in the hummocks, far above the reach of any tide". Mr H. Donnelly stated "she was in loose sand on the edge of the grassy flats, broadside on her stern". All stated that she lay so far inland behind a low hummock she could not be seen by anyone passing along the beach.

At the time of the discovery there were three Aborigines about eighty years of age, who had lived most of their life in the neighbourhood, but were unable to say how the wreck came to be there. They claimed it was there when they were children and had always looked the same.

There was, however, a tradition among the local Yangery tribe of "yellow men" having once come among them, but when or where they came from, or where they went, no one could say. However, it appeared that the Aborigines did not connect these visitors with the wreck. Captain Mills always believed these yellow men had a link with the wreck and were either Spanish or Portuguese.

Mr J. Lynar, postmaster at Belfast, often spoke of Jim Cain, a local pure-blooded Aboriginal who had two wives. One, named Kitty, was a pure Aboriginal. The second, Nellie, was quite different. Her colour, her hair, her features, particularly her profile all suggested some foreign strain, but not like the half castes.

In a letter to the Warrnambool Standard in 1899, Mr J. Archibald, Curator of the Warrnambool Museum, said, "There appears good evidence that the wreck occupied the same position with reference to the beach and sea level from about the year 1770, until she was last seen by Mr C. Donnelly of Smeaton in the summer of 1880. It is the unusual position of the ship, which is not in the water at all, or anywhere near it, the timbers of which she is built, and her evident antiquity, which have for fifty or sixty years attracted the attention of so large a number of persons, many of them seamen."

In 1847, the central part of the deck was still whole, according to Captain Mason, of Belfast. He described the wreck as resembling a large lighter, and believed the deck to be of mahogany or cedar.

One clue to which many attached importance, was the alleged existence of a Spanish coin bearing the date 1717, dug up from the a garden in Hamilton and said to have been carried there by natives who found it near the ship.

The following people are supposed to have examined the wreck, but it seems quite remarkable that, with the exception of Mason, all were reported by someone else as having seen it.

1836 Wreck discovered by sealers Gibb and Wilson. John and Charles Mills rowed a boat to the spot. John later said he had visited the wreck twice again between 1843 and 1847.

1840 Mr Allan noticed it sitting on the summit of a sandy hummock.

1843 Examined by H. Donnelly and the Mills brothers.

1846 J. Mason was riding along the beach towards Warrnambool when he saw the wreck. He estimated it to be about 100 tons, although the decks were gone and the hull full of sand. J. Jellie, riding in from Belfast, also saw it in the same year.

1847 J. Mills and R. Osburne examined the remains. Osburne asserted that the wreck was closer to Warrnambool than stated and not opposite Tower Hill.

1850 Mr Kell who saw it on various occasions, described it as being well inland.

1854 A. Rollo was supposed to have visited it a number of times and taken timber home for building purposes.

1860 As a girl, Mrs T. Manifold visited the wreck with some friends. She recalled that the vessel's head faced Belfast, and noted that the bulwarks were still stoutly panelled.

1862 F. Saul was fencing for the Warrnambool City Council on the common, when he noticed the wreck buried in the sand.

1865 J. Davis described her as "at the end of a gap in the hummocks and far from the sea".

1880 C. Donnelly, a farmer from Smeaton, who was the last to see her, found only a few ribs almost buried in the sand.

Others who claimed to have seen the wreck at various times were, Mr Wilson of Geelong, Mr Osburne of St. Kilda, Mr Rock of Warrnambool, Mr O'Connor and Mr Down.

Many believe the wreck to be that of an early sealing vessel or lighter, while others think she may be Dutch or Portuguese. The presence of early visitors on our shores has been discussed at length many times, as the MAHOGANY SHIP is only one of many unidentified wrecks lying buried and forgotten along the Australian coastline.

Early this century stories circulated of timber from the wreck having been used by pioneer settlers for building purposes and furniture making, but nothing was ever traced.

When Mr Archibald read a paper on the wreck's history to the Royal Geographical Society in 1891 wide interest was shown in attempts to locate it. Extensive searches in the area have so far failed to uncover any authentic material associated with the wreck although the Warrnambool Museum held what appeared to be an iron bolt and latch, dug up by T. Gilroy, an Inspector with the Public Works Department. Until the wreck is located, examined and the stories proved, the MAHOGANY SHIP must remain a legend.

Another mysterious wreck which created interest last century lay about two miles west of Warrnambool. It was a vessel estimated to be about 300 tons, and was believed by many to be the remains of an early whaler. Wedged between rocks and with most of the deck missing, it could only be approached at very low tide.

The remains of several vessels which disappeared without trace are supposed to lie somewhere off Victoria's south-western coastline.

On February 4th, 1852, the clipper ship DUKE OF BEDFORD, 720 tons, master Captain Dugdale, carrying 180 passengers, arrived in Melbourne, a city mad with gold fever. Almost immediately, the entire crew deserted to the goldfields, leaving the ship to join dozens of others swinging at anchor in Hobson's Bay without a crew. A number of passengers bound for Sydney were delayed up to four months before they were able to obtain a passage to Sydney.

After a great deal of expense, Captain Dugdale engaged a master to care for the ship, forfeited a sum of money due to him on the guarantee that he would return to England, and then spent a few months at the Bendigo diggings before settling on a farm at Queenscliff.

The DUKE OF BEDFORD finally left Melbourne for London via Adelaide loaded with wool. Recent research indicates she may not have been lost.

H.M.S. SAPPHO was the next vessel believed to have disappeared off the southern coastline. A sloop, built at Plymouth in 1837, she was a vessel of 428 tons, carrying sixteen guns, being commanded by Commander Fairfax Moresby, son of Admiral Sir Fairfax Moresby.

She left England for Australia late in 1857 and after calling at Capetown, resumed her voyage to Sydney, intending to pass through Bass Strait. She was sighted a few miles off Cape Otway on February 18th, 1858, but was not seen again. H.M.S. ELK and BOSCAWEN searched the Strait and approaches for some weeks, and more than a year later some gratings which could have belonged to a vessel of her type, were found washed up on Flinders Island.

Later in the same year the schooner TOROA, 58 tons, left Warrnambool for Melbourne with twelve passengers and cargo, but failed to arrive. Part of her cargo, a case of toys, washed up at Barwon Heads, indicated that she had probably foundered after rounding Cape Otway.

In March 1866, the schooner BITTER BEER disappeared off Cape Otway during a heavy gale while on a voyage from Melbourne to Belfast. A few weeks later the Warrnambool Examiner reported, "The BITTER BEER has never been seen or heard of since she left Melbourne for Port Fairy on March last. On last Monday week a bottle was picked up on the beach at Portland within which was a paper with the following words written thereon, 'Schooner BITTER BEER, black lookout'."

The ketch FOAM, 30 tons, built in 1877, owned by the Anderson family of Lorne, and skippered by the eldest son, William, disappeared off Bream Creek on January 30th, 1880, during a regular trading voyage between Loutit Bay (Lorne) and Melbourne. She weighed anchor in fine conditions, but apparently ran into a squall and foundered. Her crew of three and a boy passenger were not seen again, although a few days later a lifebuoy and wreckage washed ashore.

Two years later, in May 1882, the brig BAT, 194 tons, disappeared during a voyage from Belfast to Sydney. She was last seen near Cape Otway and S.S. DESPATCH searched for her without success.

Another mystery with a difference relates to the loss of a French whaler near Cape Nelson in 1841.

On March 10th, a large quantity of wreckage was found on the beach near Port Fairy, but judging by its condition it seemed probable that the vessel may have been lost during the winter storms of 1840. A party from Portland which searched the beach, found vast quantities of candles and the page from a French nautical almanac, dated 1838, along with other pieces which led local authorities to assume she was a French whaler of about 400 tons. The master of the cutter LIVELY, reported that he had observed smoke fires on shore during the winter, but rough seas had prevented a thorough investigation.

Then, in November 1842, when the FOX called at Portland, her master, Captain Irvine, stated that in May 1840, his ship exchanged signals with a French whaler near Kangaroo Island. He saw her again off Cape Northumberland.

Some time before this, Captain Irvine heard while in Adelaide that a French ship had landed provisions at Holdfast Bay, intending to call for them later. They were never collected.

8 – Visitors' Guide

Although the passage of time has taken a heavy toll of the remains and few surviving relics of ships lost on the West Coast, those interested may still recall a few passages of our maritime history at several points along the coast.

A simple cairn on the Bluff at Barwon Heads, dedicated by the descendants of Josiah Bean, a passenger on the EARL OF CHARLEMONT, commemorates the wreck and the pioneering spirit of the survivors. Other relics from this ship include a teapot, displayed in the Barwon Heads Hotel and an anchor raised by the Barwon Grove Skindiving Club.

After the ship SUSSEX was lost near Bream Creek in 1871, a bell from her was presented to the church at Connewarre, then moved to another church, before being erected on the grounds of the Barwon Heads Methodist Church in 1890.

Anchors from the JOSEPH H. SCAMMELL are on display at Torquay, but the most interesting relic is a house, "The Scammell" at Pride Street, built basically from the deck house, and still in first class order.

When portion of the ship containing the deck house was washed ashore, a local pioneer, W. Pride, purchased the remains for £40 and had the deck house placed on its present site using horses and rollers. The building was retained as a living room and an additional floor was erected above for bedrooms. Portion of the original appearance has been obscured by weatherboards, but the narrow doorways and portholes remain, along with some scroll work and a number of fittings. It has been classed "D" by the National Trust of Australia; that is; interesting, preservation desirable.

Anchors have been set up beside the road at Airey's Inlet and Lorne, while a visit should also be made to the grave at Godfrey Creek on the Ocean Road, near Wye River.

Apollo Bay has many items of marine interest. In addition to relics from the CASINO, CITY OF RAYVILLE and exhibits of the Historical Society, a major attraction is the carronade on display in the local museum.

Believed carried by the barque GRANGE, it had lain beneath the sea for more than 100 years when discovered by G. Anderson in Easter, 1968. After a thick layer of marine encrustation had been removed, it was found that the cast iron had changed to a very soft compound of iron oxide and carbon; so soft that it could be scraped away with one's fingernails. In this condition it was a casting of powder without strength or hardness and if left in the atmosphere, would have crumbled away. Chemical treatment brought the skin of the gun back to a hard surface, which has a ring of cast iron when struck. Restoration was carried out by Glen S.R. Walker of M. & T. Products Pty. Ltd., while the carriage crafted by G. Hamilton, is as faithful to the original as possible.

Other items, including anchors, are also undergoing restoration at Apollo Bay.

Remains from ERIC THE RED are still visible at the lighthouse reserve and Point Franklin on the Otway Peninsula. Follow the Cape Otway road to the Crayfish Bay turn, about two miles on the Apollo Bay side of the Lighthouse Reserve. At Crayfish Bay, walk east towards the Parker River. Wreckage is embedded in rocks on the eastern side of Point Franklin and is accessible at low tide. Portion of the ship is sometimes visible in the mouth of the Parker River.

Visitors to the lighthouse should ask their guide to point out the reef where the vessel was wrecked. It is covered to a depth of ten feet and extends for more than a mile south from the shore.

The small cemetery about a mile north from the lighthouse is almost obliterated by sand but contains several graves of interest. Turn right at the Lighthouse Reserve gate and follow the track through the sand hills for about a quarter of a mile, until a wire fence is seen on the left. Cross the fence and walk west over the hill. The cemetery is hidden in the next hollow.

One headstone recalls a disaster at nearby Blanket Bay on March 21st 1896, when a boat from the tender LADY LOCH, landing supplies for the lighthouse, was upset in the breakers and three members of the crew drowned. Only one body was recovered and interred in the Otway Cemetery.

Some miles west of the Ocean Road, about midway between Lavers Hill and Princetown, the turn off to Moonlight Head is clearly marked. This road leads to some of the most spectacular and historically interesting coastline in Victoria.

After leaving the Ocean Road, drive for about three kilometres to the junction of several tracks. Turn left to visit the small cemetery with its fine entrance and surrounds constructed by the late Frank Gilbert, master stonemason and tiler of Yuulong. Return to the junction and turn sharp left past the remains of the racecourse to the steps which lead down to Wreck Beach, famous for its wreck remains and gemstones. A walk of about 800 metres west from the steps brings the visitor to the anchors of the MARIE GABRIELLE embedded in the rocks. Another 400 metres to the west are anchors from the barque FIJI.

The grave of several sailors drowned at this wreck stands on the cliff above. The headstone may be reached after a difficult walk overland or by climbing the cliff above Wreck Beach. To reach the headstone from the beach, climb the steep west side of Wreck Creek, the second small creek from the steps. It enters the sea about midway between the two anchors.

To the east the remains of a wrecked barge lie on the sand, battered by the heavy seas which roll in on this section of coast. It was in tow between Adelaide and Geelong in 1935 when it broke adrift in a storm and was washed ashore. Access to this wreck is difficult, and little now remains.

Loch Ard Gorge is the focal point for the Peterborough, Port Campbell and Princetown districts. Here, in the cemetery overlooking the ocean, lie the bodies of those recovered after the tragic loss of the LOCH ARD, and also the remains of Jane Shields, Eva Carmichael's companion at Glenample, while she recovered from the terrible shock of losing her parents, brothers and sisters.

Gazetted in 1889, the cemetery originally covered about five acres, but when the National Parks Authority took control in 1964 it was closed to public burials.

The cave where Tom Pearce sheltered is at the eastern end of the gorge and Eva Carmichael's cave may be entered at low tide from the western corner.

A few miles to the east Glenample Station still stands, now restored.

Although the movement of sand has removed all traces of wrecks in the Warrnambool area, a few relics remain.

Some confusion exists as to whether the schooner ENTERPRISE, wrecked in Lady Bay in 1850 was the same vessel which took Fawkner from Tasmania to establish a settlement at Port Phillip in 1835, but a plaque in the porch of St Johns Presbyterian Church indicates that it was furnished as a memorial to the vessel.

Flagstaff Hill Maritime Villiage also holds many items of interest.

In 1856, bells from the wrecked SCHOMBERG were presented to the Catholic and Presbyterian churches, but about twelve months later the bell in the Catholic church cracked and was replaced. It lay forgotten for a number of years, then was presented to the Museum.

Other items of interest include a wooden sword supposed part of the figurehead of ERIC THE RED, timbers from ships, books and letters relating to the LOCH ARD, also miscellaneous material associated with the MAHOGANY SHIP.

To gain some idea of the mammoth task confronting would-be searchers for the MAHOGANY SHIP, turn off the highway near Tower Hill and drive to the coast. The endless rolling sand dunes should help you understand why the remains of this mysterious wreck will probably never be rediscovered.

For years a small signal cannon at the entrance to the Mechanics' Institute, Port Fairy, reminded visitors that the brig SIR JOHN BYNG was lost nearby in 1852, and a splendid memorial incorporating the propellor of the CASINO stands near the wharf.

However, apart from the restored buildings of the Belfast & Koroit Steam Navigation Company, the swinging basin in the river and the occasional uncovering of wreckage along the beach, little remains.

A similar story may be told at Portland. One of the district's earliest relics of shipwreck stands near White's Beach, Cape Bridgewater. It is near here that bodies recovered from the wreck of the MARIE were buried and a cairn now marks the spot.

The town's most noteworthy memorial commemorates an event which took place many miles to the west around the coast in South Australia. An early Portland lifeboat recalls the heroic rescue of survivors from the wrecked S.S. ADMELLA in 1859.

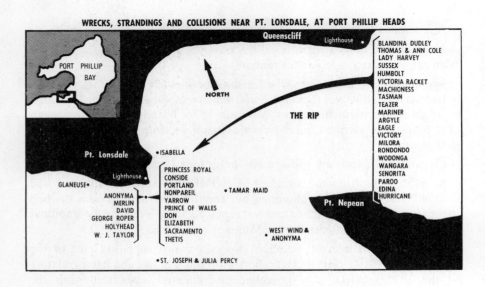

WRECKS, STRANDINGS AND COLLISIONS NEAR PT. LONSDALE, AT PORT PHILLIP HEADS

DIVERS, SHIPWRECKS ON THE VICTORIAN
WEST COAST ARE PROTECTED
UNDER COMMONWEALTH AND STATE
HISTORIC SHIPWRECKS LEGISLATION

9 – Notes to Skindivers

"Notes to Skindivers" has been compiled following discussions with many divers, but appreciation is expressed to Stan McPhee of Warrnambool in particular for information and advice on details of some of the most interesting and accessible wrecks along the West Coast.

Intending explorers should seek local knowledge wherever possible.

The Commonwealth is entitled to all wrecks found to which no owner establishes a claim. A reasonable amount of salvage is payable to a person who renders services in recovering a wreck.

"Wreck" includes jetsam, flotsam, lagan and derelict found in or on the shores of the sea, or any tidal water, and any articles or goods of whatever kind which belong or came from any ship wrecked, stranded or in distress, or any portion of the hull, machinery or equipment of any such ship.

Where any person finds or takes possession of a wreck within the limits of Australia, or having found or taken into possession any wreck outside Australia, subsequently brings it within the limits of Australia he shall give notice to the receiver, stating that he has found or taken possession of the wreck, and describing the marks by which it may be recognised.

There is no law which prevents a skindiver exploring a wreck, but he should not attempt to recover relics before ascertaining who owns the vessel. Anything recovered should be declared to the Receiver of Wrecks as soon as possible. He will treat all subsequent claims sympathetically but a heavy fine may be imposed if the law is broken and items of value concealed. If in doubt consult experienced skin divers or contact the authorities.

ANTARES

How to get there: Access is through private property. Seek local advice for exact position. Turn off the Peterborough–Warrnambool road at the cream brick church about 19 kilometres west of Peterborough.

Location of the wreck: According to Ray McDowell, who has visited her from Stanhope's Bay several kilometres to the west, she lies about 250 metres from the cliff. About ten metres of the bow can be seen from the shore in favourable conditions.

General: The remains appear to have been scattered with the fore section well to the west of the main hull. Other wreckage includes three anchors, rudder, windlass, large square iron boxes, yellow metal, iron work and red tiles. If descending directly to the wreck down a crevice cut by a small watercourse, ropes are necessary.

ANT

Location of the wreck: Believed to lie on a reef about four kilometres west of Barwon Heads, now known locally as the Ant Spit, which is covered to a depth of four metres with its outer edge about a kilometre offshore.

General: Although the remains of the boiler were visible from the beach for many years, the exact site of the wreck has been lost. Few relics have been recovered but it is possible the hull of the vessel might still be intact.

CASINO

How to get there: Select a fine, calm day. Ascend Marriner's Lookout north of Apollo Bay. Look due east. If sand has not covered the wreck its shape will be seen on a calm, sunny day about 400 metres from the shore. In calm weather the ship may also be seen from a boat.

Location of the wreck: In about seven metres of water a short distance offshore near the Cable Station.

General: The boilers, stern and most of the keel were intact until recently. Pieces of the ship lie scattered over a wide area. Many interesting relics have been recovered, including portholes, anchors and sundry ship fittings.

EARL OF CHARLEMONT

How to get there: Turn at the Barwon Heads Hotel corner and drive slowly through the camping park to the top of the Bluff.

Location of the wreck: About 200 metres W.S.W. from the Bluff. Unfortunately a movement of sand covers the remains periodically.

General: Anchors, chains, hatches, rails and portion of a mast still lie in about four metres of water. Articles recovered include an anchor, bottles, cutlery and crockery.

ERIC THE RED

How to get there: Follow the Cape Otway road to Crayfish Bay, turn a short distance on the Apollo Bay side of the lighthouse reserve. At Crayfish Bay walk east towards the Parker River. Wreckage lies scattered on the beach and buried in the sand.

Location of the wreck: The ship struck on the outer edge of the Otway Reef more than two kilometres south of Cape Otway, but heavy seas and strong currents make it virtually inaccessible with present equipment.

General: This wooden vessel disintegrated and large pieces of wreckage drifted ashore at many points. The bow section was thrown up on Point Franklin and profitable diving could probably be carried out off the rocks under favourable conditions.

FALLS OF HALLADALE

How to get there: Turn off the Ocean Road at the western edge of Peterborough and follow the Bay of Islands tourist road to the eastern end of Massacre Bay. About 500 metres from the junction take the left turn and proceed to Wreck Point.

Location of the wreck: About 300 metres south from the point.

General: The hull has collapsed and the decks have gone. A jumble of metal work, sections of masts and spars, railings and anchors lie scattered over a wide area. There are also several interesting holes to explore.

GEORGE ROPER & HOLYHEAD

How to get there: Leave the car in the lighthouse reserve at Point Lonsdale and proceed on foot to the base of the lighthouse.

Location of the wrecks: They lie close together on the Lonsdale Reef in a south to south-easterly bearing, about 400 metres from the lighthouse.

General: Both of these vessels were partially salvaged when lost but divers have recovered crockery, glassware, bottles and numerous fittings. The Rip is a very dangerous area for inexperienced divers.

GRANGE

How to get there: Drive south from Apollo Bay to Marengo. Walk to Point Haley near the abandoned quarry and look east.

Location of the wreck: Although the exact location of this wreck is now lost it is believed that the GRANGE struck near the most easterly point of the larger reef in the channel between the two masses of rock.

General: Several small vessels have been lost here, making it difficult to identify any particular wreck. Major items recovered include a carronade and anchor.

INVERLOCHY

How to get there: The reef where the ship was lost is best seen from Demon's Bluff north-east from Anglesea.

Location of the wreck: On the seaward side of Ingoldsby Reef which lies about two kilometres east of Anglesea. The reef consists of two rocks above low water surrounded by sunken rocks on which the sea breaks heavily.

General: Skindivers have recovered a wide variety of relics including crockery, bottles and ship fittings.

JOSEPH H. SCAMMELL

How to get there: Point Danger is south of Torquay and easily accessible.

Location of the wreck: Remains of the ship lie about 300 metres off shore E.S.E. from Point Danger.

General: Divers have recovered many relics including three anchors.

LA BELLA

Location of the wreck: On La Bella Reef near the Warrnambool breakwater.

General: Little remains of the ship but some railway iron, scattered ballast and section of a mast may be located.

LOCH ARD

How to get there: The turn to the gorge is clearly signposted a few kilometres east of Port Campbell on the Great Ocean Road.

Location of the wreck: A short distance off the south-west point of Mutton Bird Island (approximately 500 metres). Seek local advice.

General: Stand on the cliffs overlooking the entrance to the blowhole. To the south-east is the point on the island near where the vessel struck. Warrnambool skindiver, Stan McPhee located the wreck in 1967 and since then a large quantity of lead, copper, bronze, crockery, bottles and other fittings have been recovered. Now badly damaged by illegal blasting, the hull has broken in two; the upper deck and hull are missing down to the lower deck.

MARIE GABRIELLE & FIJI

How to get there: Turn off the Great Ocean Road at the Moonlight Head signpost and proceed with care to the head of the steps leading down to Wreck Beach.

Location of the wrecks: Approximately opposite the two groups of anchors lying on the beach, the MARIE GABRIELLLE being about 500 metres west from the foot of the steps and the FIJI a further 400 metres along the beach.

General: Rough seas common in this area have battered these vessels and destroyed most items of interest or value.

NAPIER

How to get there: In Port Campbell Bay.

Location of the wreck: Stand on the jetty and look to the cliffs opposite. At low tide a little of the boiler may be seen although it has now rusted and collapsed. An anchor and chain lie submerged about 30 metres seaward.

NEWFIELD

How to get there: As for the SCHOMBERG. Climb to the point on the left of the turntable. The vessel was lost in the small bay to the left and her remains now lie about 100 metres off shore. Nothing is visible.

General: Portholes, pieces of the ship and yellow metal have been recovered.

ORUNGAL

How to get there: A sighting on the wreck may be made from the Bluff at Barwon Heads. Turn at the Barwon Heads hotel and drive through the camping area to the top of the Bluff.

Location of the wreck: About one kilometre E.S.E. from the Bluff.

General: This wreck has been pounded off the reef where it originally lay, but the four boilers still stand erect and may sometimes be seen at low tide. Apart from the anchors and a few sundry items most fittings have been recovered.

SCHOMBERG

How to get there: Turn off the Great Ocean Road at the Timboon signpost about a kilometre east of Peterborough and drive to the cliff edge. To the south-west the Schomberg Rock stands well out of the sea, particularly at low tide when the sand spit may be easily seen.

Location of the wreck: Although the vessel supposedly grounded a short distance to the left of the rock, her remains were recently discovered about 900 metres out to sea.

General: Most of her woodwork has gone but the shape of the vessel remains, composed of rails, girders and her frame. Items recovered include portion of the rudder, tubing, bolts, plumbing fittings, Muntz metal sheeting, copper nails, crockery and sundry items of cargo.

SPECULANT

How to get there: Park the car in a safe area beside the Great Ocean Road about 400 metres west from the Cape Patten sign and descend the nearby track which leads directly to the beach. A more direct route leads down from the lookout but should be taken with great care.

Location of the wreck: Directly below the lookout.

General: The widening of the Great Ocean Road has covered relics from the ship with many tons of rock. The careful diver might locate pieces from the ship beside the rocks in calm seas. An anchor recovered by the Underwater Explorers is now displayed on the Apollo Bay foreshore.

SUSSEX

Location of the wreck: Off Bancoora Beach.

General: The wreck has disintegrated but a number of fittings lie scattered over a wide area. Anchors also lie nearby.

VICTORIA TOWER

Location of the wreck: Approximately four kilometres N.E. by E. from Point Danger.

General: Wreckage is scattered over a wide area about 300 metres off shore. The patient diver may locate brass fittings and some iron plate. Among the items already recovered are bottles, slates, anchors and other ship fittings.

W.B. GODFREY

How to get there: Godfrey River is on the Great Ocean Road about three kilometres east of Wye River.

Location of the wreck: The ribs and anchor of the vessel are visible and accessible at very low tide. A second anchor and more of the ship lie further out in deeper water, beyond the line of breakers.

General: Being easily accessible most relics have been recovered from this wreck.

WOLLOMAI

How to get there: Off the Great Ocean Road about three kilometres south of Apollo Bay.

Location of the wreck: Four hundred metres north along the beach from Haley Reef.

General: Although normally covered by sand to a depth of two metres, strong easterlies occasionally scour out the beach, when it is then possible to examine a winch and stand on the remains of the hull at low tide.

WRECKS IN APOLLO BAY

The construction of the breakwater and a heavy build-up of sand has covered the remains of vessels lost on the town beach and lost cannon balls believed used as ballast in timber lighters. Several unidentified anchors lie offshore in deep water.

WRECKS IN LOUTIT BAY

Many years ago the remains of most wrecks were bulldozed from the beach. Scouring of sand, particularly near the mouth of the Erskine River, occasionally exposes a few pieces of wreckage.

WRECKS AT PORT FAIRY

Early charts and maps show the approximate location of the major wrecks but a heavy build-up of sand has obliterated most traces. Occasionally wreckage is uncovered within easy swimming distance from the shore. Items recovered include anchors, chains, bells, bottles, rope, fittings, remnants of clothing, brass and copper bolts, timber, crockery, knives, forks, spoons and whale bones.

WRECKS AT PORTLAND

Major alterations to the port have removed most remains although divers might discover items of interest in the area close to the lighthouse.

WRECKS IN LADY BAY, WARRNAMBOOL

Sanding of the harbour has covered the remains of wrecks to depths exceeding ten metres.

10 – Collisions & Strandings

Few ships escaped after driving ashore on open sections of the inhospitable West Coast, but many of those which stranded in the partially sheltered small harbours and bights were eventually refloated and repaired.

The most interesting and notable incidents are described here, while full lists of all collisions and groundings are set out in the appendices.

EARLY STRANDINGS

An examination of early records shows that the first recorded stranding occurred near Portland in 1834. On September 11th the Launceston Advertiser reported that the schooner HENRY was anchored waiting to load whale oil when driven ashore by a gale. She was later refloated.

Five years later the schooner MINERVA also went ashore near Portland and was subsequently refloated, beached, then repaired.

Ships entering and leaving Port Phillip Bay also joined the lists of early casualties. On February 24th, 1841, the barque ARGYLE, inward bound from London, went ashore near Point Lonsdale and was not refloated for five days, while a few days later the schooner EAGLE was stranded nearby.

1845

The schooner TEAZER, first seagoing vessel built on the banks of the Yarra, bound for Portland, ran ashore near Point Lonsdale on March 20th but floated off after throwing ballast overboard.

1846

Ten passengers reached safety along a line after the schooner WAVE was driven on to the beach at Port Fairy on October 13th. She was refloated a fortnight later only slightly damaged.

1847

Suspicious circumstances surrounded the stranding of the schooner CLARENCE at Warrnambool on September 11th after she apparently parted her anchor. Refloated, she went ashore again at Port Fairy on November 19th.

1849

The cutter WILLIAM was the first vessel in serious trouble along the Otway coastline. She was anchored in Loutit Bay loading timber for Geelong when heavy seas parted her anchors and she drifted on to the beach, where she remained upright in the sand until refloated, and sailed back to Geelong for repairs.

1850

Victory Shoal, near Point Lonsdale, takes its name from the barque VICTORY which stranded there on August 15th, 106 days out from Glasgow with

103

50 passengers. After throwing some cargo overboard and discharging the remainder into lighters, she was towed off and taken to Melbourne for repairs.

1851

On January 3rd, while entering The Rip on her inward voyage from London with 25 passengers, the barque TASMAN, 562 tons, refused to answer her helm in the strong tide and was swept on to the Lonsdale Reef. Hauled free, she was towed to Hobson's Bay, making several inches of water per hour.

1853

The schooner COLINA and the ship DANIEL SHARP collided west of Cape Otway after the DANIEL SHARP had approached to confirm her position. The COLINA's main boom and stern were badly damaged but she sailed on to Portland for repairs.

1854

The American ship HUMBOLT, 700 tons, went ashore near Point Lonsdale when attempting to enter Port Phillip Bay without a pilot on March 1st. She was freed three days later.

1855

The barque MATADOR, 295 tons, collided with S.S. QUEEN, 207 tons, two miles off Cape Patten on the night of December 12th. Both vessels were extensively damaged but reached port. S.S. QUEEN was a well known steamer employed in the West Coast trade.

1856

The ship THOMAS & ANN COLE, 800 tons, inward bound, struck the Lonsdale Reef on January 14th and was badly holed. She was towed free the following day and taken to Melbourne making more than two feet of water per hour.

1860

The celebrated S.S. GREAT BRITAIN, in the final hours of a voyage out from England, collided with S.S. OSCAR in the early hours of September 21st west of Port Phillip Heads. Both ships suffered considerable superficial damage but were not in any real danger.

S.S. LADY BIRD, popular West Coast steamer, parted her anchor cables during a storm at Portland on February 11th and was driven ashore north of the jetties while her engine room crew battled desperately to raise steam. She was refloated practically undamaged four days later.

1863

S.S. EDINA, Australia's most famous steamer, had three narrow escapes while operating on the West Coast. On April 18th, 1863, she was at anchor in Portland Bay when a squall sprang up and forced her ashore where she lay for two days, battered by heavy seas, before being refloated and taken to Melbourne for repairs.

When entering Port Phillip Heads on the morning of April 30th, 1869, on a voyage from Warrnambool to Melbourne with a number of passengers and a full cargo, she struck a submerged object and began taking water. The pumps were set to work until she reached Williamstown, where she was run ashore. Lieutenant Stanley, of H.M.S. PHAROS, surveyed the approaches on the Point Lonsdale side and reported that she had probably grazed the Lonsdale Reef.

During a gale at Warrnambool in 1870, the steamer DANDENONG drifted close to the EDINA and finally swung broadside on to her bow, damaging the EDINA's figurehead, which was replaced when she was overhauled during 1872-73.

1879

A gale washed the PEVERIL ashore on July 6th while she was loading at Warrnambool. She was repaired on the beach and about a month later refloated at high tide. She had just been towed clear when the towing chain broke and she was again washed ashore. After this she was abandoned by the insurance company and purchased back by her former owner who successfully effected repairs and refloated her several months later.

1879

Present day visitors to Port Campbell are often surprised when told that small trading craft regularly entered the tiny bay before the days of roads and harbour facilities.

The cutter ASIA which traded between Warrnambool and Port Campbell almost left her bones in the tiny cove on Febraury 25th, when trapped there by a storm. Huge waves eventually forced her on to the beach where local residents dragged her clear of the seas until she could be refloated. This stranding renewed local agitation for the installation of permanent government moorings and reawakened interest in the proposed jetty.

1881

A collision between the west coast steamers NELSON and JULIA PERCY off Apollo Bay at 2 p.m. on December 25th, received great publicity when compared with the LADY BIRD – CHAMPION disaster only a few kilometres away twenty-four years earlier.

Both vessels were in sight of each other for some time but for reasons never satisfactorily explained the NELSON veered into the JULIA PERCY near her funnel, buckling her plates but otherwise causing little damage. However, the NELSON sustained serious injuries having her bows stove in and stem carried away. At the moment of impact forty passengers jumped from the NELSON on to the JULIA PERCY, one man being crushed badly between the two vessels and another falling overboard and drowning. When the NELSON was later docked in Melbourne a large hole was discovered in the starboard bow.

In the same year the iron barque HEREFORD, 1,524 tons, went stern foremost on to the Ingoldsby Reef off Anglesea and stuck fast.

After some delay all the passengers were landed safely and preparations were made to salvage the vessel. On the night of January 17th, 1882, rough seas trapped some of the salvage crew on board and next morning a policeman and seamen were drowned when a wave capsized a boat carrying nineteen men from the wreck to the shore.

The HEREFORD was sold for £8,500, her cargo unloaded and she was then pumped dry before being towed clear of the reef on February 17th, 1882, after almost five months ashore.

During the tow to Melbourne she became almost unmanageable when in the vicinity of The Heads, but she eventually reached Melbourne where an examination showed that her keel and stern post had been carried away although she was not holed.

The HEREFORD ended her days under the Norwegian flag when she was abandoned at sea in April 1907.

1883

The iron steamer BERENGARIA, 1,394 tons, ran ashore west of Barwon Heads on February 3rd and her signals of distress soon attracted large groups of onlookers hoping for plunder.

Police were stationed on the beach to protect her cargo of wine, spirits, beer and general merchandise dumped into the sea, but more than 3,000 people eventually arrived on the scene and were soon in control. Large quantities of beer and spirits were stolen and buried in the sandhills while others broke open tins of preserved meat and fish. Buckets, jugs, bottles and pig tubs were filled with liquor and soon dozens of men, youths and boys were reeling over the beach.

The BERENGARIA was freed on February 5th and towed to Melbourne.

1888

The inquiry into the stranding of S.S. BOWRA at Apollo Bay on December 15th was the first investigation carried out by the newly-formed Court of Marine Inquiry.

The BOWRA lay on the beach for six days before being towed free by the tug ALBATROSS.

1891

While browsing through copies of the Melbourne Argus for 1891 my attention was drawn to the report of the death of an Indian rhinoceros at the Melbourne Zoo, believed due to the battering he had received while a passenger on the steamer BANCOORA as she lay stranded at Bream Creek for almost two months.

While being towed to Melbourne for repairs, a steel cable snagged on some rocks in The Rip and almost dragged her ashore, but she was eventually docked and repaired at a cost exceeding £20,000. Skin divers tell us one of her anchors still lies off Breamlea.

1898

Rivalry between crews almost caused a disaster off Apollo Bay early on the morning of January 3rd. Conditions were calm and clear with a smooth sea but S.S. CASINO altered course when passing S.S. FLINDERS and struck her gently amidships on the starboard side causing light structural damage.

Following an inquiry, the Marine Board charged the First Mate of the FLINDERS and Second Mate of the CASINO with misconduct.

1908

Newspapers gave confusing accounts of Captain Royan's part in the stranding of the four-masted barque HINEMOA at Lorne on January 21st.

Fierce fires had been raging in the Otways for more than a week forcing HINEMOA to sail blind through a thick smoke screen as ashes fell on her deck and myriads of birds and insects sought haven in the rigging.

Although the ship was making little headway a strong current carried her towards land until without shock she glided on to rocks near the Pacific Hotel on the edge of the town.

The news that a large ship was aground spread rapidly through the district, attracting hundreds of sightseers, but her master, Captain Royan seldom appeared on deck, spending most of his time in his cabin playing a phonograph.

Word was telegraphed to Melbourne, and when the tug EAGLE arrived to tow her free, the Chief Officer took charge until the HINEMOA was moored at Williamstown.

On January 22nd the Geelong Advertiser stated that Captain Royan became ill in Adelaide and remained there leaving a coasting pilot in charge, but the Melbourne Argus on the same day published an interview with Royan where he agreed that he had been displaced.

However, the Court of Marine Inquiry stated quite definitely that Royan was in charge between Melbourne and Adelaide.

The HINEMOA, a vessel of 2,283 tons, was torpedoed and sunk on September 17th, 1917 while on a voyage in ballast from Falmouth to New York.

1912

S.S. POTOMAC and S.S. GEORGIC collided in a dense smoky haze about eight kilometres off Cape Patten on February 8th. Damage was not serious.

SOME RECENT INCIDENTS

During this century, particularly since World War I the rapid developments in navigational aids and a steady decline in the local coastal trade, brought about by the vast improvement in road and rail transport, resulted in a great reduction in shipping incidents around the Victorian coast.

The Apollo Bay Company, formed shortly after World War I used the ketch SWALLOW to trade between Melbourne and Apollo Bay.

Early in 1922 she was struck by an easterly gale while unloading at the Apollo Bay jetty and blown ashore where she remained on the sand for several days before being refloated on a high tide.

Her loss in Port Phillip Bay a few months later terminated the company.

S.S. WANGARA stranded near Point Lonsdale in November 1961 when forced too far to the west in the main channel by an incoming vessel but she was freed and taken to Melbourne for repairs.

Incidents involving pilot vessels have been few and far between in recent years. In the collision between M.V. BASS TRADER and P.C. WYUNA in foggy conditions off Port Phillip Heads in 1972, no one was injured and both vessels suffered only minor damage.

UPDATE OF SMALL SHIP LOSSES

1852　Schooner PORTLAND lost at Point Lonsdale.
1888　Schooner MAFFRA wrecked west of Point Lonsdale.
1901　Yacht KIANGA wrecked at Warrnambool.
1933　Motor launch lost between Rye and Apollo Bay.
1948　Fishing boat LORNA lost on the Lonsdale Reef.
1967　Trawler VERONICA missing off the Otway coast.
1977　C-SHELL lost near the Fitzroy River.
1977　CROMARTY lost near Warrnambool.
1978　MIZAM lost near Apollo Bay.
1979　Fishing boat ROSE MARIE lost near Cape Nelson.
1980　Fishing boat GARDNER lost near Cape Otway.
1981　Fishing boat SARTUNA lost near Cape Nelson.
1982　Yacht RELENTLESS wrecked near Queenscliff.
1983　Fishing boat SPRAY lost on the Lonsdale Reef.
1985　Shark Cat swamped near Warrnambool. 2 lives.
1991　Trawler TAMMY R. foundered south-west of Portland.
1991　Pilot launch GEORGE TOBIN overwhelmed in The Rip.
1992　Yacht SQUIRREL foundered off Point Lonsdale.
1992　Fishing boat TURBO swamped off Ocean Grove.

11 – Flotsam & Jetsam

In marine circles "flotsam" is defined as goods found floating on the sea and "jetsam" material thrown overboard to lighten the vessel.

The flotsam and jetsam in this chapter are brief biographies of some of the outstanding personalities involved in the wrecks on the west coast and a few sidelights of interest.

CAPTAIN FORBES – SCHOMBERG

When the gold fever in Australia clutched its victims from aboard, the shipping companies vied with each other in building fast clipper ships to provide speedy passages to the new El Dorado.

During the early fifties the names of the great captains appeared – and the greatest amongst them all was James Nicol Forbes, Bully Forbes, Hell-or-Melbourne Forbes – take your pick – whose meteoric career was abruptly terminated when he lost the giant SCHOMBERG at Peterborough in 1855.

No photograph or illustration of Forbes has been preserved but he was described as being 5'6¾" tall, of ruddy complexion with brown hair and blue eyes. He carried a scar from a cut over his right eye.

Born in 1822, Forbes was apprenticed in 1833 and received his Mate's ticket when 24 years of age. While visiting Quebec he was appointed to temporary command of the ship WILSON KENNEDY, 1,129 tons, and first attracted the attention of the noted shipowner, James Baines, who appointed him as master of the barques CLEOPATRA, 421 tons, then the MARIA, 1,014 tons.

Obtaining his Master's Certificate on 11-6-1852, he made sea history as captain of the famous clipper MARCO POLO. She left Liverpool on July 4th, 1852, with 930 emigrants and a crew of 60, and made the round trip to Melbourne and back in 5 months 21 days sailing time, arriving home on March 13th, 1853, with 648 passengers – a tribute to his capacity to size up a situation and make quick, ruthless decisions.

On his arrival in Hobson's Bay he found the anchorage littered with ships whose crews had deserted to the goldfields. Forbes promptly trumped up a charge of insubordination against his own crew and had them clapped in irons until ready to sail home.

He set the seal on his fame with another quick round trip, this time giving the famous flier, KENT, five days start from Melbourne and catching her after rounding Cape Horn.

In 1854 Forbes went to Boston to take charge of the LIGHTNING and on her maiden voyage to Liverpool, sailed from Boston light to the Rock light at the mouth of the Mersey in 13 days 20 hours, including a record 24 hours run of 436 nautical miles, the best ever under sail.

In May, 1854, he took the LIGHTNING to Melbourne, arriving with many of his passengers almost hysterical with fright. Most of the great captains of his day were never afraid to carry sail, but Forbes could outsail them all. To a deputation of scared passengers who implored him to take in some of his canvas, he curtly replied that he was in sole charge and would not tolerate mutinous talk. Other stories were told of him standing over the halliards with a pistol in case anyone should attempt to let them go.

Forbes took her out to Melbourne in 77 days and home in 63 days 16 hours, then left her for the SCHOMBERG, but his luck was running out.

After losing her near Curdie's Inlet (page 8), and successfully defending the charges brought against him, Forbes returned to England on the OCEAN CHIEF, arriving on 10-5-1856.

He remained on shore for some time before Baines appointed him to the HASTINGS in 1857, but in 1858 she had to return to Sydney during a passage from Moreton Bay to Bombay. Forbes went to great pains through the Sydney press to point out that the ship was leaking badly and could be classed as unseaworthy.

He finally lost her near Algoa Bay, off the Cape of Good Hope, in December, 1859. She was found by the French barque CHEVREUIL, with seven feet of water in the hold. All the crew were taken off and landed at Table Bay, but the HASTINGS finally drifted ashore at Sunday's River and became a total wreck.

In 1862 the EARL OF DERBY from Glasgow was wrecked on the Irish coast and Forbes was sent by her owners to superintend salvage operations.

From 1863 until 1866 he was back at sea in command of the GENERAL WINDHAM from Liverpool, and in her he still managed fast passages.

In 1867 Baines gave him command of the MARCO POLO once again, but she was now well past her best and was being used more as a general trader. Forbes remained with her until she was sold in 1871.

His career at sea finished, Forbes retired to Liverpool where he died on June 13th, 1874, at the comparatively early age of 52. He had married in 1855 between leaving the LIGHTNING and taking over the SCHOMBERG, but his wife predeceased him by almost ten years, dying on September 26th, 1864.

CAPTAIN FAWTHROP – HARBOUR MASTER AT PORTLAND

A dominant figure in many shipwreck rescues while Harbour Master at Portland, Captain Fawthrop was born at Plymouth, England, in 1804 and first visited Australia as an officer on a convict ship in 1829. He returned in 1834 and spent 15 months in the pilot service at Tamar Heads in northern Tasmania.

In 1835 he took charge of the EAGLE and in 1837 Henty engaged him to take sheep to Portland. Other vessels he commanded were the schooner MINERVA, brig JULIA PERCY and the brig CITY OF SYDNEY.

He was appointed Harbour Master at Portland in 1853 and retired on half pay in 1868, dying in 1878 at the age of 74.

Fawthrop achieved fame during the rescue of survivors from the ADMELLA on the South Australian coast in 1859, but he also organised rescue crews for wrecks around Portland.

A short time after his appointment as Harbour Master, Fawthrop led a party of men who cut the cables on the burning emigrant ship NEW ZEALANDER and allowed her to drift ashore where she burnt to the water's edge (page 8).

Next, he played a leading role in the arrest of suspects believed responsible for the sinking of the barque NESTOR (page 33).

On June 7th, 1863, a report reached Portland that a ship was ashore west of Cape Bridgewater. Fawthrop immediately sent the rocket crew overland and also despatched the lifeboat by sea, then supervised all rescue attempts (page 37).

Two months later, on August 2nd, he was in charge of the lifeboat when called to rescue the crew of the brig JULIA, seen in distress near the Fitzroy River (page 81). Shortly after the crew transferred to the lifeboat the brig drifted ashore and became a total wreck. It was here that the crew of a whaleboat which also went to the rescue were drowned when it capsized.

Historians are indebted to Fawthrop, whose well-kept records have provided a detailed description of an important period in Portland's history.

CAPTAIN HART - ISABELLA

The career of Captain Hart, master of the barque ISABELLA, which was lost near Portland in 1837 (page 26), shows him to have been one of the most picturesque and versatile seafaring men in the colony.

Born in England in 1809, he first went to sea at the age of 12 and arrived in Hobart in 1828. After serving as mate on several vessels, he entered the Australian coasting trade before spending portion of the early 1830s sealing and whaling in Bass Strait.

In 1838 Hart overlanded 500 cattle from Darlot's Creek to Adelaide, then resumed whaling in the early forties before settling in Adelaide and building a flour mill in 1846.

He entered politics and was elected to the Legislative Council as a member for Victoria in 1851, then to the Assembly for Port Adelaide in 1857, Light in 1868 and Burra in 1870. He was a member of nine ministries and Premier on three occasions between 1865 and 1871. Hart died in 1873.

CAPTAIN JEFFERY - MASTER MARINER

Captain Jeffery, who lost the schooner SEABIRD near Apollo Bay in 1895 (page 88), was one of the best known trading masters around the Otway coast during the days of sail, possessing considerable knowledge of the Otway weather and tides, often displaying great skill and daring in the handling of his craft.

Born in England in 1858, Jeffery arrived in Australia in 1893 and served on vessels in the Bass Strait island trade before becoming captain of the coastal trader ROVER in the Melbourne to Apollo Bay trade.

After marrying, he settled in Apollo Bay and when he lost the SEABIRD, used a lighter to unload from S.S. CASINO before the jetty was extended. Other vessels he skippered included the CENTURION, ALICE, SWALLOW, LIALEETA and ERSKINE. Jeffery died in 1941.

CAPTAIN MIDDLETON – CASINO

Although steamers had operated regularly around the West Coast since the early 1850s, it was not until the wreck of S.S. CASINO at Apollo Bay in 1932 that Captain John Middleton became the first master of a steamer on the run to die in a shipwreck (page 70).

Captain Middleton, who had been master of the CASINO for several years, was born in Glasgow but came to Australia in 1905 and entered the service of the Union Steamship Company.

Later, after some years as master on vessels of the Newcastle and Hunter River Steam Navigation Company on the north coast of N.S.W., he transferred to the CASINO.

CAPTAIN A.R. PLEACE

Born in England in 1828, Captain Pleace had a lifelong association with the sea before losing his life near Lorne in 1891.

Most of his early years were spent at sea and during this time he was involved in one major shipping incident near Portarlington.

While inward bound from Brisbane to Melbourne with Captain Pleace in command, the brigantine CHALLENGER, 300 tons, was run down and sunk by S.S. AVOCA on October 26th, 1870, fortunately without loss of life.

In 1871 he was appointed to the Pilot Service and a few months later the Pilot Board of Victoria issued him with a full Pilot's Licence for the Port of Geelong. He also held the position of Geelong Harbour Master for a short period before moving to Albert Park, then returned to the sea as an officer in the inter-colonial trade. His next position was as chief mate on the barquentine CHITTOOR and he was serving in this position when drowned during salvage operations on the W.B. GODFREY.

On the morning of Saturday, April 18th, while Pleace was steering a boat from the shore out to the wreck, it was capsized by a heavy sea, throwing the five occupants, Pleace, Weir, Watts, McIntyre and Hangard, into the water. They managed to right it but after it capsized again three times, decided to abandon further attempts and swim to safety.

Weir and Pleace clung to a lifebuoy for some time until Pleace seized a floating oar and struck out for the wreck. A line was thrown to him but the sea threw him against the side of the ship and he apparently struck his head. Another seaman on the wreck dragged him ashore but he did not respond.

McIntyre was also drowned when he apparently became entangled in kelp.

112

PERCY HOLDEN

During a 44-year association with the Customs Department which commenced at Geelong in 1883, Mr Percy Holden was called upon to attend all wrecks on the coast from Queenscliff to Lorne, and this provided him with many exciting and varied experiences.

When the HOLYHEAD was wrecked at Point Lonsdale in 1890, Mr Holden remained at the wreck for three months, living on board until it showed signs of breaking up. There was no jetty at Point Lonsdale in those years and the Customs officers went backward and forward by dinghy from the wreck to the reef. On one occasion he and another officer were proceeding to the HOLYHEAD when the dinghy's oars snapped in two, leaving the men adrift in the notorious Rip. The lighthouse-keeper signalled to two fishermen who were making for Queenscliff in their boat and a rescue was effected. Both Customs officers were surprised to find that their rescuers were two men whom they had prosecuted a week previously for smuggling whisky from the wreck.

Plunderers at the remains of the JOSEPH SCAMMELL forced Mr Holden, three mounted police and several constables to camp on the beach to protect the cargo as it washed ashore. Police were also stationed at the bridge over the Barwon River at Geelong but many still smuggled goods out of the district.

Mr Holden's keen interest in ships led him to record facts concerning more than 950 wrecks on the south-eastern coast of Australia.

TWO NARROW ESCAPES

The only sailing vessel of any size to attempt the narrow passage between Lawrence Rocks and the mainland near Portland was the brig CORNELIUS in 1854.

A brig of 350 tons, master Captain Clarke and drawing 20 feet of water, she left for London with an unfavourable wind, forcing her master to attempt the narrow passage or run her ashore. She passed through with her false keel torn off.

Then, in January, 1878, S.S. NELSON, on a bay excursion to celebrate the opening of the Hamilton to Portland railway and carrying 300 distinguished passengers, passed between the Lawrence Rocks. In the swell she bottomed twice, throwing her passengers to the deck, but then passed through without further incident.

FAILURE OF LOCH ARD SALVAGE

Several syndicates and individual speculators amassed considerable fortunes salvaging shipwrecks but the most successful salvager on the West Coast, James Miller, lost heavily on the wreck of the LOCH ARD when he confidently expected it to net him his greatest profit.

Miller, who was born in England in 1837, arrived in Australia in 1853 and entered the hotel trade in Geelong until 1882 when he turned his attention to the buying of shipwrecks, achieving success with the salvage of several near Port Phillip Heads, namely the SUSSEX and VICTORIA TOWER; also the LOCH LEVEN on King Island.

Miller and two others purchased the wreck of the LOCH ARD for £2,120 but only succeeded in recovering a small portion of the cargo before rough seas washed most of it away. Also, S.S. NAPIER, which he had chartered for salvage work, ran ashore at Port Campbell and was destroyed by a gale when almost refloated. The partnership was dissolved but Miller did not relinquish ownership of the wrecked LOCH ARD, thus giving his descendants the opportunity to claim it when rediscovered almost 90 years later.

Miller's other interests included brickmaking and he was also a director of the Corio Bay Steam Yacht Company Limited, which planned to run excursions around the bay, but never materialised.

Miller retired to Malvern and died there in 1894.

LIFE SAVING BY ROCKET

Numerous rocket stations were established on the West Coast last century at a time when many vessels were meeting disaster, often after a long voyage through the roaring forties and almost in sight of their destination.

A small mortar fired the line carrying rocket across the ship. The line was fastened to a tailed block with an endless fall rove through it. The block was made fast to the ship's mast, then those on shore hauled a stout hawser out to the ship. The instructions for fastening the rocket line to the ship were set out on a board in four languages as follows: "Fasten tail block to lower mast well up; if masts gone, then to best place handy; cast off rocket line; see rope on block runs free; show signal to shore."

As soon as the hawser reached the shipwrecked crew they made it fast and the people on shore hauled it tight as possible, making an aerial ropeway between ship and shore.

The breeches buoy was then hauled off to the ship, using the endless fall and the shipwrecked crew were hauled one by one through the surf to safety. Although a clumsy and awkward method of life saving, many lives were saved using this technique.

EARL OF CHARLEMONT COMMEMORATION

In a unique gathering on November 14th, 1953, eighty descendants of Josiah Bean, who as a young man of 23 survived the wreck of the CHARLEMONT one hundred years earlier, joined in a thanksgiving service at All Saints Church of England, Barwon Heads, and later attended the unveiling of a memorial cairn on The Bluff dedicated to the pioneering spirit of the survivors.

The cairn, erected by the Shire of South Barwon, was unveiled by the Shire President, Cr. G.A. Cameron, the bronze tablet being provided by Josiah Bean's descendants.

Josiah and Charles Bean both landed from the wreck, Charles settling at Geelong while his brother searched for gold at Woods Point and Red Hill near Castlemaine.

After the gold rush subsided the brothers established a flour mill and later Josiah farmed in the Mallee and entered the building business in Melbourne.

He died in 1910 in his 81st year. His wife whom he met in Australia survived him by twelve years.

OWNERSHIP AND PROFIT FROM A VOYAGE

Registry acts governed the ownership of ships which would be registered in "sixty fourths". That is, 64 shares in the ship would be sold with one person usually owning a large share. The EARL OF CHARLEMONT, wrecked at Barwon Heads, was owned thus:

William Carvill of Newry, in Ireland, a merchant – 56/64 shares

William Garner, of Newry, a shipmaster – 8/64 shares.

Garner was the ship's master.

When the JOSEPH H. SCAMMELL was built in Nova Scotia in 1884 she had six owners holding the 64 shares. John Walter Scammell, of New York, held 47 shares and the man after whom the ship was named, Joseph H. Scammell, held four shares. Some shares changed hands over the next seven years and the owners of the ship when she was lost at Torquay were:

John W. Scammell, merchant – 47/64 shares

Joseph H. Scammell, merchant – 4/64 shares

William F. Harrison, merchant – 3/64 shares

Joseph F. Merritt, merchant – 1/64 shares

John Thompson, merchant – 6/64 shares

John A. Chapman, master mariner – 3/64 shares.

Chapman was the ship's master.

At the end of each voyage the owners published full details which included statements of costs. Profits would be divided in proportion to the number of shares held.

Here is a summary of profits on each voyage made by the ill-fated LOCH ARD:

Voyage 1 – Glasgow to Melbourne and return to London:

Earned £11,274 freight.   Gross profit on voyage: £2,792.

Cost of feeding crew: 1/6 per man per day.

Voyage 2 – London to Melbourne and return:

Earned £8,933 freight.   Gross profit on voyage: £1,500.

Cost of feeding crew: 1/3 per man per day.

Voyage 3 – London to Calcutta and return:

Earned £8,383 freight.   Gross profit on voyage: £2,645.

Cost of feeding crew: 1/5 per man per day.

Voyage 4 – Glasgow to Melbourne and return to London via Calcutta:

Earned £9,655 freight.   Gross profit on voyage: £1,385.

Cost of feeding crew: 1/4 per man per day.

Voyage 5 – Uncompleted (wrecked near Port Campbell):

Freight and passage money collected: £3,823.

Insurance premium paid by owners to cover vessel: £647.

OUT OF THE PAST

Glenample homestead, close to the Great Ocean Road west of Princetown, is poignant with memories going back almost a century when hundreds of curious sightseers, reporters and officials travelled many miles over rough tracks to meet the tall, sad-faced, quiet Irish girl, Eva Carmichael, resting after a miraculous escape from the wreck of the iron clipper LOCH ARD and the tragic loss of her family.

It was here that pioneer settler Hugh Gibson and his wife did all in their power to alleviate her suffering, sheltering her from the publicity-hungry people attempting to exploit her misfortune.

Following the LOCH ARD disaster the publicity the area received caused Gibson great hardship, when selectors moved in, horses were stolen, sheep killed and fences cut. To make matters worse the Government refused to recognise the station boundaries and restricted the run to one mile back from the sea. Gibson eventually relinquished his share in the property and moved to Mulwala.

A few kilometres to the east stood Rivernook Guest House, where accommodation was outstanding and hospitality a byword, inextricably linked with the Evans family.

Visitors from all over Victoria went there year after year, never deterred by the arduous journey over rough tracks, knowing that at the end lay a happy holiday.

Rivernook's greatest hour came in 1891 when the barque FIJI was wrecked nearby, for it was to the guest house that the survivors were carried, to be rested and restored to health.

"Rivernook" Evans, as he was widely known, had many relics from this and other wrecks and he delighted in yarning about them in front of a great fire of Otway logs, at night, when the air grew keen.

It is sad now to return to the site of the old homestead, a flattened area on a knoll overlooking the Gellibrand River, within sound of the sea. All that remain are a few scattered timbers, broken fences and twisted trees.

Another famous landmark holding links with the sea was Jeffery's Fernery Hotel, established in 1856 by Thomas Jeffery at the north-west corner of Aphrasia Street and the West Melbourne Road (now Shannon Avenue) in Newtown, Geelong.

Among the attractions in the fernery, attached to the hotel, were relics from shipwrecks around the Australian coast, including a number from vessels lost along the West Coast.

These included a ship's ladder from the JOSEPH H. SCAMMELL, ship's wheel from the SUSSEX and lifebuoys from the LOCH ARD and SOUTH MILTON.

Thomas Jeffery died in 1887 and the hotel was carried on by his son until 1895, when Hodges Brothers Breweries took over. Nothing remains today but nearby Fernery Grove off Aphrasia Street commemorates its existence.

THE BLANKET BAY DISASTER

On the morning of March 21st, 1896, supplies for the Otway lighthouse were being landed at Blanket Bay by boat from the lighthouse tender LADY LOCH when an immense roller upset the boat, spilling the seven occupants into the sea. None were wearing life jackets.

Able Seaman Monks disappeared immediately but the remainder were washed on to a reef near the entrance and watched helplessly as a second boat was despatched to their assistance.

Meanwhile, Ordinary Seaman Mathieson was washed away and drowned while Mate Griffiths, who seemed dazed, swam away from his rescuers and disappeared.

Monk's body was found about 300 metres to the east next morning but the others were not recovered. His body was interred in the Otway Cemetery and a headstone erected to those who lost their lives.

It reads:

Albert Griffiths – Chief Officer, 33.
Thomas Monks – Able Seaman, 34.
Alex Mathieson – Ordinary Seaman, 23.
Lost their lives in the Blanket Bay Disaster, 21st March, 1896.

A MYSTERY FROM THE SCHOMBERG

Did wreckage from the clipper SCHOMBERG drift across the Tasman to Taupeickaka Creek on the West Coast of the South Island of New Zealand?

Remains discovered by gold miners using the beach for a road in the 1860s were identified as part of the ship, after a Captain McIntyre had several pieces sent to Melbourne on S.S. OTAGO and examined by the Inspector of Telegraphs for Victoria, who claimed to know the SCHOMBERG and was prepared to swear the wreckage was from her.

From time to time others confirmed his identification, basing their claims on the type of construction and the fact that apparently no vessel of this size with diagonal planking, certain types of timbers and wooden trenails had been lost in New Zealand waters up until the time of discovery.

More than 100 years later, when a road had been opened close to where the wreckage lay, Baden Norris, of Christchurch, visited the site and found the remains buried deep in the mud of a lagoon. He was not certain it was part of the SCHOMBERG but believed it was the remains of a vessel with five skins of diagonal planking, felt lined between each skin.

The modern name for the creek where the wreckage lies is Ship Creek, probably named after the wreckage.

APPENDIX A

STRANDINGS

1834 Schooner *HENRY* (near Portland).
1839 Schooner *MINERVA* (near Portland).
1841 Barque *ARGYLE* (near Point Lonsdale).
1841 Schooner *EAGLE* (near Point Lonsdale).
1843 Brig *DIANA* (Portland).
1843 Schooner *MINERVA* (Port Fairy).
1845 Schooner *TEAZER* (near Point Lonsdale).
1845 Cutter *MARINER* (near Point Lonsdale).
1846 *WAVE* (Port Fairy).
1846 Brig *WILL WATCH* (Portland).
1847 Schooner *CLARENCE* (Warrnambool).
1848 Barque *TENASSERIM* (near Point Addis).
1848 Schooner *JANE* (near Warrnambool).
1849 Cutter *WILLIAM* (Loutit Bay).
1850 Barque *VICTORY* (near Point Lonsdale).
1850 Schooner *WAVE* (Port Fairy).
1850 Cutter *WILLIAM* (Apollo Bay).
1850 Schooner *MARGARET* (Apollo Bay).
1851 Barque *TASMAN* (near Point Lonsdale).
1852 Brigantine *MARY & AGNES* (Port Fairy).
1852 Schooner *PEARL* (Port Fairy).
1853 Ship *VICTORIA PACKET* (near Point Lonsdale).
1853 Brigantine *MARCHIONESS* (near Point Lonsdale).
1853 Brig *TRITON* (Port Fairy).
1854 Brig *LADY HARVEY* (near Point Lonsdale).
1854 Ship *HUMBOLT* (near Point Lonsdale).
1854 Schooner *ALERT* (Port Fairy).
1854 Schooner *PEARL* (Port Fairy).
1856 Ship *THOMAS & ANN COLE* (near Point Lonsdale).
1856 Schooner *HELEN* (near Point Lonsdale).
1856 Brig *CHRISTINA* (Apollo Bay).
1857 Schooner *VICTORY* (near Point Lonsdale).
1857 Schooner *HIGHLANDER* (Apollo Bay).
1858 Schooner *ANNE* (near Apollo Bay).
1860 *S.S. LADY BIRD* (Portland).
1860 Schooner *EVA* (Portland).
1863 *S.S. EDINA* (Portland).
1863 Schooner *JULIET* (Port Fairy).
1863 Sloop *PEVERIL* (Warrnambool).
1863 Barque *SUSSEX* (near Point Lonsdale).
1864 Ship *BLANDINA DUDLEY* (near Point Lonsdale).
1866 Brigantine *AQUILA* (Warrnambool).
1868 Brig *MARY GRANT* (Port Fairy).
1868 Brigantine *ELIZA GODDARD* (Port Fairy).
1868 Brigantine *DART* (Warrnambool).
1869 *S.S. EDINA* (near Point Lonsdale).

1871　Schooner *CAROLINE* (Port Fairy).
1873　Pilot Schooner *RIP* (near Point Lonsdale).
1873　Schooner *ORWELL* (Port Fairy).
1876　Schooner *MINNA BELL* (Portland).
1877　*S.S. ARGYLE* (Warrnambool).
1877　*S.S. LUBRA* (Warrnambool).
1878　*S.S. NELSON* (near Cape Otway).
1879　Cutter *ASIA* (Port Campbell).
1880　Schooner *TRADER* (Warrnambool).
1881　Schooner *FLORENCE* (Portland).
1881　Barque *HEREFORD* (near Anglesea).
1882　Schooner *LOUISA* (Port Fairy).
1882　*S.S. COORONG* (Curdie's Inlet).
1883　*S.S. RODONDO* (near Point Lonsdale).
1883　*S.S. BERENGARIA* (near Barwon Heads).
1884　Schooner *UNITY* (Apollo Bay).
1885　*S.S. BELLINGER* (near Anglesea).
1888　*S.S. BOWRA* (Apollo Bay).
1889　Barque *RACHEL* (Warrnambool).
1891　*S.S. BANCOORA* (Breamlea).
1891　Schooner *ENDEAVOUR* (Breamlea).
1892　*S.S. WODONGA* (near Point Lonsdale).
1892　Lugger *ROVER* (Blanket Bay).
1894　*S.S. CASINO* (Moyne River).
1898　*S.S. INNAMINCKA* (near Cape Otway).
1898　Ketch *WELLINGTON* (Breamlea).
1900　Ketch *ELSINORE* (Apollo Bay).
1902　*S.S. PAROO* (near Point Lonsdale).
1908　Barque *HINEMOA* (near Lorne).
1912　*S.S. LEURA* (Warrnambool).
1916　Barquentine *SENORITA* (near Point Lonsdale).
1920　*S.S. GILGAI* (near Barwon Heads).
1922　Ketch *SWALLOW* (Apollo Bay).
1924　*S.S. CASINO* (near Kennett River).
1929　*S.S. CASINO* (Warrnambool).
1934　*S.S. MILORA* (near Point Lonsdale).
1934　*S.S. CORAMBA* (Warrnambool).
1938　*S.S. WANNON* (Portland).
1940　Ketch *PENGANA* (near Portland).
1961　*S.S. WANGARA* (near Point Lonsdale).

APPENDIX B.
MINOR COLLISIONS

1853 S.S. *WEST WIND* and Pilot Schooner *ANONYMA* (off Heads).
1853 Schooner *COLINA* and Ship *DANIEL SHARP* (off Cape Otway).
1855 Barque *MATADOR* and S.S. *QUEEN* (off Cape Patten).
1857 Brig *GERTRUDE* and Ship *GENERAL NOWELL* (off Cape Otway).
1860 S.S. *OSCAR* and S.S. *GREAT BRITAIN* (near Cape Otway).
1870 S.S. *DANDENONG* and S.S. *EDINA* (Lady Bay, Warrnambool).
1879 Ship *ST JOSEPH* and S.S. *JULIA PERCY* (off Heads).
1881 S.S. *NELSON* and S.S. *JULIA PERCY* (off Apollo Bay).
1889 Ship *SARDOMENE* and Ketch *VISION* (off Warrnambool).
1898 S.S. *FLINDERS* and S.S. *CASINO* (off Apollo Bay).
1912 S.S. *GEORGIC* and S.S. *POTOMAC* (off Cape Patten).
1972 M.V. *BASS TRADER* and P.C. *WYUNA* (off Heads).

APPENDIX C.
LOSSES OF LIGHTERS AND BARGES

1866 Lighter *RESULT* (at Curdie's Inlet).
1880 Lighter *OTWAY* (at Warrnambool).
1884 Lighter *GAZELLE* (at Apollo Bay).
1935 Unnamed barge (at Moonlight Head).

APPENDIX D.
HEAVIEST LOSS OF LIFE

1878 *LOCH ARD* (near Port Campbell), 49 lives.
1839 *CHILDREN* (at Childers Cove), 38 lives.
1857 *CHAMPION* (off Cape Otway), 32 lives.
1852 *DUKE OF BEDFORD* (south-west of Cape Otway), 30+ lives.
1858 *H.M.S. SAPPHO* (east of Cape Otway), 30+ lives.
1852 *CONSIDE* (at Point Lonsdale), 14 lives.
1891 *FIJI* (at Moonlight Head), 12 lives.
1932 *CASINO* (at Apollo Bay), 10 lives.
1892 *NEWFIELD* (at Peterborough), 9 lives.
1905 *LA BELLA* (at Warrnambool), 7 lives.

ANTARES, wrecked west of Peterborough, 1914.

APPENDIX E.
MAJOR LIGHTS

Cape Nelson
Built 1884. Reconditioned 1934.
Light 250 feet (76 metres) above sea level, 608,000 candle power, visible 22 miles (35½ kilometres).
Description: A white tower with a red band, 79 feet (24 metres) high.

Whaler Point Portland Bay
Built 1889. Reconditioned 1920.
Unattended light 135 feet (41 metres) above sea level, visible for 15 miles (24 kilometres).

Griffith Island
Built 1855. Reconditioned 1955.
Light 41 feet (12 metres) above sea level, visible for 11 miles (18 kilometres).
Description: White circular tower, 36 feet (11 metres) high.

Warrnambool Bay
Built 1871. Reconditioned 1917.
Light is the rear light in a two-light system, 109 feet (33 metres) above sea level, visible 11 miles (18 kilometres), 200 candle power.
Description: White stone structure.

Cape Otway
Built 1848. Reconditioned 1939.
Light 300 feet (91 metres) above sea level, 1,000,000 candle power, visible 24 miles (39 kilometres).
Description: White circular tower, 62 feet (19 metres) high.

Split Point
Built 1891. Reconditioned 1919.
Unattended light, 218 feet (66 metres) above sea level, 7,000 candle power, white light, visible 20 miles (32 kilometres). Red, visible 9 miles (14½ kilometres).

Point Lonsdale
Built 1867. Reconditioned 1919.
Light 120 feet (37 metres) above sea level, 4,000 candle power. White light visible for 17 miles (27½ kilometres). Red, 8 miles (13 kilometres).
Description: White concrete tower, 70 feet (21 metres) high.

APPENDIX F.
WRECKS ON THE RIVERS

Sandbars block the mouths of all rivers but there have been two major disasters.

1898
The passenger steamer PERSEVERANCE was leaving the Glenelg River in February to trade on the Murray River when she struck a sandbar and lost her propeller. Her crew reached safety but she soon became a total wreck.

1921
The sinking of the launch NESTOR in the Hopkins River on January 9th was one of the worst disasters ever to occur in the Warrnambool district.

Licensed to carry 83 passengers, she left from the lower reaches for Jubilee Park with a near capacity load of mainly women and children, but after travelling about two kilometres upstream sprang a leak and became unmanageable.

A line was passed to three boys in a boat to be fastened to the bank but it slipped from their grasp and the launch slowly settled in deep water amid scenes of confusion.

Many rescue boats hurried to the scene and helped people from the water, but ten lost their lives.

APPENDIX G.
CHRONOLOGICAL LIST OF WRECKS

Pre-1800   Mahogany Ship. Between Warrnambool and Port Fairy.
1836   *SARAH ANN* (cutter), Port Fairy.
1837   *ISABELLA* (barque), Cape Northumberland.
1837   *THISTLE* (schooner), Port Fairy.
1838   *CHILDREN* (barque), Childer's Cove.
1839   *MARIA* (schooner), Portland.
1840   *MARY ANN* (barque), Port Fairy.
1840   *MARY* (barque), Portland.
1841   Unknown whaler, near Portland.
1841   *ISABELLA* (cutter), Point Lonsdale.
1842   *DUSTY MILLER* (schooner), Port Fairy.
1842   *TRUGANINI* (schooner), Warrnambool.
1843   *THOMAS* (cutter), Port Fairy.
1843   *JOANNA* (schooner), Joanna River.
1843   *SOCRATES* (barque), Port Fairy.
1844   *ELIZABETH* (schooner), Port Fairy.
1844   *SALLY ANN* (schooner), Port Fairy.
1844   *DIANA* (brig), Port Fairy.
1846   *ELIZABETH* (brig), Portland.
1846   *SQUATTER* (schooner), Port Fairy.
1847   *LYDIA* (barque), Port Fairy.
1848   *THETIS* (schooner), Point Lonsdale.
1849   *PRINCESS ROYAL* (barque), Point Lonsdale.
1849   *MINERVA* (schooner), off Cape Otway.
1849   *SARAH LOUISA* (brig), Port Fairy.
1849   *LADY MARY PELHAM* (brig), Portland.
1850   *CAPTAIN COOK* (schooner), Portland.
1850   *DAVID* (schooner), Point Lonsdale.
1850   *ENTERPRISE* (schooner), Warrnambool.
1851   *MARIE* (barque), Cape Bridgewater.
1852   *ELIZABETH* (schooner), west of Cape Otway.
1852   *ESSENDON* (brig), Port Fairy.
1852   *DUKE OF BEDFORD* (ship), west of Cape Otway.
1852   *LILLIAS* (schooner), Warrnambool.
1852   *MARY JANE* (schooner), Portland.
1852   *CONSIDE* (steamer), Point Lonsdale.

1852   *MARGARET & AGNES* (brigantine), Portland.
1852   *SIR JOHN BYNG* (brig), Port Fairy.
1853   *EARL OF CHARLEMONT* (ship), Barwon Heads.
1853   *SACRAMENTO* (ship), Point Lonsdale.
1853   *NEW ZEALANDER* (ship), Portland.
1853   *ARCHER* (barque), Warrnambool.
1853   *FREEDOM* (schooner), Warrnambool.
1853   *HENRY* (schooner), Portland.
1853   *MEROPE* (barque), Portland Bay.
1854   *JENNY* (brig), west of Cape Otway.
1854   *COLUMBINE* (brig), Ocean Grove.
1854   *OSPREY* (schooner), Lorne.
1854   *ANNA* (brigantine), Apollo Bay.
1854   *INELLAN* (barque), Port Fairy.
1854   *DUNDEE* (barque), Port Fairy.
1854   *NESTOR* (barque), Portland.
1855   *CONSTANT* (barque), Portland.
1855   *AUSTRALASIA* (barque), Portland.
1855   *SWIFT* (schooner), Port Fairy.
1855   *REBEL* (schooner), Lorne.
1855   *SCHOMBERG* (ship), Peterborough.
1856   *ELANORA* (brig), Apollo Bay.
1857   *CHAMPION* (steamer), off Cape Otway.
1857   *NONPAREIL* (schooner), Point Lonsdale.
1857   *ANNIE* (schooner), Apollo Bay.
1857   *VICTORY* (schooner), Portland.
1858   *LADY HARVEY* (brig), Barwon Heads.
1858   *JOHN SCOTT* (brig), Flaxman's Hill.
1858   *H.M.S. SAPPHO* (sloop), east of Cape Otway.
1858   *MARTHA* (schooner), Point Franklin.
1858   *TOROA* (schooner), off West Coast.
1858   *GRANGE* (barque), Apollo Bay.
1859   *MAID OF JULPHA* (brig), Warrnambool.
1859   *ANONYMA* (schooner), Point Lonsdale.
1860   *TAMORA* (barque), Portland.
1860   *ELIZABETH* (schooner), Point Lonsdale.
1861   *HERCULES* (brigantine), Apollo Bay.
1861   *PRINCE OF WALES* (schooner), Point Lonsdale.
1862   *TUBAL CAIN* (ship), south-west of Cape Otway.
1862   *OTWAY* (schooner), Lorne.
1863   *ANNE* (schooner), Lorne.
1863   *JANE* (barque), Cape Bridgewater.
1863   *JULIA* (brig), Portland.
1863   *GOLDEN SPRING* (brig), Warrnambool.
1864   *FAIR TASMANIAN* (brig), Warrnambool.
1866   *BITTER BEER* (schooner), off Cape Otway.
1866   *ANT* (steamer), Bream Creek.
1866   *ELIZA* (schooner), Port Fairy.

1867   *BLACK WATCH* (schooner), off Cape Otway.
1867   *LADY ROBILLIARD* (schooner), Portland.
1868   *LIGHT OF THE AGE* (ship), Ocean Grove.
1868   *PHOENIX* (ketch), Ocean Grove.
1868   *LUCY LEE* (cutter), Bream Creek.
1868   *BALMORAL* (brigantine), Portland.
1869   *VICTORIA TOWER* (ship), Bream Creek.
1869   *MARIE GABRIELLE* (barque), Moonlight Head.
1870   *YARROW* (brig), Point Lonsdale.
1871   *SUSSEX* (ship), Bream Creek.
1871   *BARWON* (steamer), Cape Bridgewater.
1872   *MARY CUMMINGS* (schooner), Cape Patten.
1875   *DON* (schooner), Point Lonsdale.
1876   *WATER LILY* (schooner), Port Fairy.
1877   *YOUNG AUSTRALIA* (schooner), Peterborough.
1878   *LOCH ARD* (ship), Port Campbell.
1878   *HENRY* (ketch), Lorne.
1878   *NAPIER* (paddle steamer), Port Campbell.
1880   *FOAM* (ketch), Bream Creek.
1880   *ERIC THE RED* (ship), Cape Otway.
1882   *BAT* (brig), off West Coast.
1882   *MIRANDA* (schooner), Apollo Bay.
1882   *OLIVIA DAVIS* (barque), Warrnambool.
1882   *SWAN* (ketch), Apollo Bay.
1882   *ALEXANDRA* (brig), Warrnambool.
1882   *YARRA* (brigantine), Warrnambool.
1882   *JANE* (brigantine), Warrnambool.
1883   *GEORGE ROPER* (barque), Point Lonsdale.
1883   *ALEXANDER* (cutter), Apollo Bay.
1886   *PAUL JONES* (ship), off Lorne.
1886   *SOUTH MILTON* (barque), Barwon Heads.
1886   *GLANEUSE* (barque), Point Lonsdale.
1887   *GANGE* (barque), Point Lonsdale.
1888   *EDINBURGH CASTLE* (barque), Warrnambool.
1888   *EMILY* (ketch), Joanna River.
1889   *TRADER* (schooner), Lorne.
1890   *ALBERT* (ketch), Lorne.
1890   *HOLYHEAD* (barque), Point Lonsdale.
1891   *W.B. GODFREY* (barque), Godfrey River.
1891   *JOSEPH H. SCAMMELL* (barque), Torquay.
1891   *FIJI* (barque), Moonlight Head.
1892   *NEWFIELD* (barque), Peterborough.
1894   *FREETRADER* (barque), Warrnambool.
1894   *W.J. TAYLOR* (ketch), Point Lonsdale.
1895   *SEABIRD* (schooner), Cape Patten.
1897   *KELPIE* (tug), off Heads.
1902   *INVERLOCHY* (barque), Anglesea.
1905   *LA BELLA* (barquentine), Warrnambool.

1908 *FALLS OF HALLADALE* (barque), Peterborough.
1911 *SPECULANT* (barquentine), Cape Patten.
1914 *ANTARES* (steamer), Bay of Islands.
1923 *WOLLOMAI* (schooner), Apollo Bay.
1925 *LIALEETA* (ketch), off West Coast.
1929 *SELJE* (steamer), off Cape Otway.
1932 *CASINO* (steamer), Apollo Bay.
1940 *CITY OF RAYVILLE* (motor vessel), off Cape Otway.
1940 *ORUNGAL* (steamer), Barwon Heads.
1954 *BLACK WITCH I* (schooner), Apollo Bay.
1958 *BLACK WITCH II* (schooner), Apollo Bay.

APPENDIX H.
WORST YEARS

The rush of emigrants anxious to seek their fortunes on the Victorian goldfields brought out ships crowded with passengers. Many of these disappeared without trace or were lost when almost within sight of their destination.

The worst years for shipwrecks on the West Coast were:

    1858 – 7 wrecks.
    1852 – 6 wrecks.
    1853 – 6 wrecks.
    1854 – 6 wrecks.
    1882 – 6 wrecks.
    1849 – 5 wrecks.
    1855 – 5 wrecks.

Remains of W.B. GODFREY at low tide.

APPENDIX I.
VESSELS INVOLVED IN RESCUES AND INCIDENTS
AT WRECKS ON THE WEST COAST

Wreck of SACRAMENTO

The Government schooner EMPIRE worked as a pilot vessel and assisted at wrecks at Port Phillip Heads. Other duties included maintenance of buoys and beacons, also the carrying of stores.

P.S. APHRASIA entered the Melbourne–Geelong trade in 1841 and traded in Port Phillip Bay until she left for New Zealand, where she was wrecked in 1864.

Wreck of EARL OF CHARLEMONT

The Pilot schooner ANONYMA, 42 tons, commenced at Port Phillip Heads in 1853 and was in service until wrecked west of Point Lonsdale in 1859.

The schooner BOOMERANG, 99 tons, took up duty as a pilot vessel in 1852 but was not a complete success.

Wreck of SCHOMBERG

S.S. QUEEN, 207 tons, commenced in the West Coast trade in 1853.

Wreck of LIGHT OF THE AGE

Tug WARHAWK, 59 tons, built 1865. Broken up 1901.

Tug RESOLUTE, 134 tons, built 1858. Broken up 1925.

Tug TITAN, 97 tons, built 1866. Sold to New Zealand interests.

Cutter BEN BOLT was used by Captain Leggett, a well-known pioneer in the coastal trade in many of his salvage assignments.

RESULT, ketch of 27 tons, built in 1864.

PHOENIX was a vessel of 24 tons which was returning from the wreck when lost near Point Lonsdale.

Wreck of VICTORIA TOWER

Tug TITAN (see LIGHT OF THE AGE).

Wreck of SUSSEX

Tugs WARHAWK and TITAN (see LIGHT OF THE AGE).

Tug CHALLENGE, built in 1856. Transferred to Newcastle in 1874 and broken up in 1917.

Tug MYSTERY, 21 tons, built 1876. Removed from register in 1928.

Wreck of LOCH ARD

S.S. NAPIER (see page 57).

Wreck of ERIC THE RED

S.S. DAWN, 522 tons, operated around the West Coast from 1877 until 1898, finally being condemned and sunk at Suva in 1928.

S.S. OTWAY, 563 tons, operated regularly around the West Coast from 1873 until 1878 and then transferred to inter-colonial run between Melbourne and Adelaide. Broken up 1919.

H.M.V.C.S. VICTORIA, 580 tons, spent 20 years employed by the Victorian Government searching for lost ships, surveying unknown waters, laying cable, supplying remote lighthouses and finally finishing as a bay steamer. She was dismantled in 1895.

S.S. PHAROS, 156 tons. A tug in Port Phillip Bay. Broken up in 1934.

The schooner APOLLO was built at Apollo Bay using timbers salvaged from the wreck. She traded in Victorian and Tasmanian waters.

Burning of PAUL JONES
Iron clipper ANTIOPE, 1,400 tons, built 1866. Hulked after World War I.

LIGURIA, 2,993 tons, built 1874. Broken up at Genoa 1903.

S.S. NELSON, 649 tons. Employed in the West Coast trade from 1876 until 1890. Lost in the Tamar River soon after transferring to Tasmanian run.

S.S. DEPATCH, entered the bay trade in 1869 and then served as a Government steamer until 1893 when she commenced to operate around the Gippsland coast. Lost at Lakes Entrance in 1911.

Wreck of CHILDREN
Barque SOCRATES, 152 tons (see page 31).

Schooner SALLY ANN, 52 tons, wrecked 1844 (see page 84).

Wreck of DUNDEE
Ship BENJAMIN ELKIN, built 1849, 425 tons.

Wreck of GRANGE
Tug LIONESS, built 1854. Paddle steamer of 26 tons net, 87 tons gross. Wrecked at Greymouth, New Zealand, 1882.

S.S. MOEGAERA.

Wreck of OLIVIA DAVIS
Barque PROSPECTOR, 235 tons, built 1878.

Wreck of GEORGE ROPER
P.S. WILLIAMS, 327 tons, built in 1854 and broken up 1894. Used as an excursion steamer and tug.

S.S. DAWN (see ERIC THE RED).

P.S. ALBATROSS, 191 tons. A tug built in 1875.

S.S. BLACK BOY, 66 tons, built 1857.

S.S PHAROS, 156 tons, built 1881. Broken up 1934.

S.S. FLEETWING, 31 tons, built 1874. Broken up 1894.

Schooner AGNES, 20 tons, built 1872.

S.S. CLEOPATRA, 200 tons, converted to lighter.

S.S. SPRAY, 393 tons, built 1872.

Wreck of SOUTH MILTON
The Pilot schooner RIP, 92 tons, joined the service in 1860.

Wreck of GLANEUSE
Tug AVON, 110 tons, built 1868.

Wreck of EDINBURGH CASTLE
S.S. JULIA PERCY, 580 tons, was a famous West Coast steamer at intervals from 1876 until 1903. Scuttled in Bass Strait in 1934.

Wreck of HOLYHEAD
P.S. ALBATROSS (see GEORGE ROPER).

Ketch LU LU, 43 tons, built at Belfast and registered in Melbourne. Rammed and sunk by S.S. EXCELSIOR in 1897 but refloated.

Tug PILOT, 39 tons.

Wreck of W.B. GODFREY
Ketch JESSIE (fishing boat).
S.S. LADY LOCH, 487 tons, built in 1886. She was employed in the Lighthouse Service. Hulked in 1934.
S.S. RACER, a tug of 185 tons, built in 1886. Broken up in 1934.
Barque CHITTOOR, 217 tons, built in 1875 and registered in Sydney.
Schooner CLARA, 28 tons, built in 1870 and registered in Melbourne.

Wreck of FIJI
S.S. LADY LOCH (see W.B. GODFREY).
S.S. RACER (see W.B. GODFREY).

Wreck of NEWFIELD
S.S. JULIA PERCY (see EDINBURGH CASTLE).

Wreck of CONSIDE
P.S. MAITLAND, 140 tons, built in 1837. Wrecked in New Zealand waters in 1865.

Sinking of CHAMPION
S.S. MELBOURNE, 115 tons, built 1852. Lost at the mouth of the Murray River in 1859.
S.S. LADY BIRD, 420 tons, built 1851. Scuttled in Cook Strait in 1905.

Wreck of ANT
S.S. SAMSON, tug of 75 tons. Lost in New Zealand waters.

Sinking of SELJE
S.S. KAITUNA, 2,042 tons, built 1904.
S.S. EAGLE, tug of 229 tons, built 1890. Broken up 1960.

Wreck of CASINO
S.S. EAGLE (see SELJE).
S.S. BATMAN, tug of 338 tons, built 1883.
S.S. CORAMBA, 531 tons, built 1911. She foundered near Phillip Island 1934.

Sinking of CITY OF RAYVILLE
M.V. PINGUIN, 7,766 tons. This German raider built in 1936 sank or captured 28 ships before being sunk on 8-5-1941.
S.S. STORSTAD (PASSAT), 8,998 tons. Captured by Germans 7-10-1940. Lost in air attack 1942.
S.S. CAMBRIDGE, 10,846 tons, built 1916.
H.M.S. CORNWALL, 9,800 tons, built 1928. Reconstructed 1936. Main armament eight 8″ guns.
H.M.A.S. ORARA, built 1907. Saw war service as a minesweeper 1939–1945. Sold to Chinese interests 1948. Sunk 1950.

Wreck of ORUNGAL
S.S. ORMISTON, 5,832 tons, built 1922.

Wreck of TRUGANINI
P.S. SEAHORSE, 540 tons, built in 1837. Used by Benjamin Boyd for the coastal trade. Badly damaged in the Tamar River, Tasmania, in 1843. Auctioned 1849. Hulked 1850.

Wreck of ELIZABETH
COLINA, 55 tons, built 1848.

Wreck of LADY ROBILLIARD
PHILIPPINE.

Wreck of MARY CUMMINGS
P.S. MYSTERY (see SUSSEX).

Wreck of JENNY
Government brig PACIFICO, 146 tons, built 1854.

Wreck of COLUMBINE
Pilot schooner BOOMBERANG (see EARL OF CHARLEMONT).

Wreck of LADY HARVEY
Steam tug LIONESS (see GRANGE).

Burning of MAID OF JULPHA
Sloop PEVERIL, 71 tons.

Wreck of YARROW
Tug MYSTERY (see SUSSEX).

Wreck of YARRA
S.S. DAWN (see ERIC THE RED).

Wreck of JOANNA
Cutter BARBARA.

Wreck of BLACK WATCH
S.S. COORONG, 304 tons, built 1862. Hulked 1911.
Wreck of ALBERT
Pilot schooner RIP (see SOUTH MILTON).

Disappearance of H.M.S. SAPPHO
H.M.S. ELK, a sailing vessel of 12 guns attached to the East India Station, which included Australia.
H.M.S. BOSCAWEN.

Disappearance of BAT
S.S. DESPATCH (see PAUL JONES).

APPENDIX J.
SUMMARY OF DETAILS OF FAMOUS SHIPS
MENTIONED IN THIS BOOK

DONALD MACKAY: Built 1855. 2486 tons. Best 24-hour run 421 nautical miles. Finished as a coal hulk at Madeira.

DOVER CASTLE: Built 1858. 1003 tons. Broken up.

JAMES BAINES: Built 1854. 2275 tons. Burnt at Liverpool in 1858.

LIGHTNING: Built 1854. 2096 tons. Best 24-hour run 436 nautical miles. Burnt at Geelong, Victoria, in 1869.

LOCH SUNART: One of the famous Loch Line. Built 1878. 1231 tons. Wrecked on the Irish coast 1879.

LOCH VENNACHAR: One of the famous Loch Line. Built 1875. 1485 tons. Wrecked near Kangaroo Island 1905.

MADAGASCAR: Built 1837. 835 tons. Disappeared after leaving Melbourne for London 1853.

MARCO POLO: Built 1852. 2039 tons. Best 24-hour run 428 nautical miles. Wrecked in Canadian waters 1883.

THERMOPYLAE: Built 1868. 948 tons register. Sunk off Lisbon 1907.

TORRENS: Built 1875. 1276 tons register. Broken up 1910.

KENT: Built 1853. 927 tons. Hulked.

OCEAN CHIEF: 1026 tons register. Burnt at Bluff, New Zealand, 1862.

APPENDIX K.

ORIGINS OF NAMES OF WEST COAST PORTS AND PRINCIPAL COASTAL FEATURES

APOLLO BAY: Settled 1850. Named after a schooner which sheltered there during a voyage from Melbourne to Warrnambool.

CAPE BRIDGEWATER: Grant named it in honour of the third and last Duke of Bridgewater.

CAPE NELSON: After Grant's ship LADY NELSON.

CAPE OTWAY: Named by Grant after his friend William Albany Otway, R.N.

CAPE PATTEN (Patton): After Admiral Patton, later Lord of the Admiralty.

JULIA PERCY ISLAND: In honor of Lady Julia Percy, a member of the Northumberland family.

LAWRENCE ROCKS: After Captain Lawrence.

LOUTIT BAY: Settled 1849. Named after Captain Loutit, who traded around the Otway coastline and later took the first ship-load of wool to England. Renamed Lorne in 1870 after the Marquis of Lorne.

MOONLIGHT HEAD: Flinders saw it in moonlight between squalls.

POINT LONSDALE: After Captain William Lonsdale.

PORT CAMPBELL: Named after Captain Campbell, an early whaler.

PORT FAIRY: Named after the whaling cutter Fairy. For a time known as Belfast.

PORTLAND BAY: After the Duke of Portland.

WARRNAMBOOL: Settlement developed here in the forties.

DIVERS, SHIPWRECKS ON THE VICTORIAN
WEST COAST ARE PROTECTED
UNDER COMMONWEALTH AND STATE
HISTORIC SHIPWRECKS LEGISLATION

Surveyors examine the gaping hole in the bows of the KAITUNA after she collided with and sank the SELJE, 1929.

131

The clipper SCHOMBERG, lost near Peterborough, 1855.

Blanket Bay, scene of the 1896 disaster when 3 crewmen from the lighthouse tender LADY LOCH lost their lives.

Collision of the TUBAL CAIN and CONSTANCE south west of Cape Otway, 1862.

Wreck of the VICTORIA TOWER near Bream Creek, 1869.

Salvagers at work on the SUSSEX near Barwon Heads, 1871.

The barque GANGE ashore at Point Lonsdale, 1887.

The barque FREETRADER a total wreck at Warrnambool, 1894.

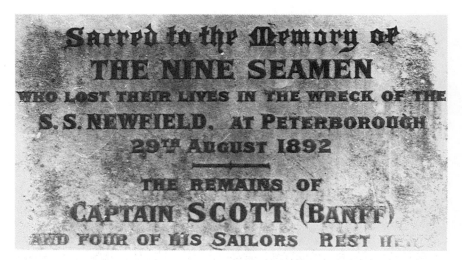

Sacred to the Memory of
THE NINE SEAMEN
WHO LOST THEIR LIVES IN THE WRECK OF THE
S. S. NEWFIELD, AT PETERBOROUGH
29TH AUGUST 1892
———
THE REMAINS OF
CAPTAIN SCOTT (BANFF)
AND FOUR OF HIS SAILORS REST HERE

Inscription on the headstone above the grave of sailors lost on the Newfield.

The WOLLOMAI ashore near Apollo Bay, 1923.

INDEX – SHIPS

PLACES

Aberdeen: 79
Adelaide: 19, 29, 32, 54, 57, 58, 64, 70-73, 76, 80-83, 86, 91, 92, 94, 107, 111
Airey's Inlet: 56, 93
Aire River: 33
Anglesea: 49, 65, 99, 106
Apollo Bay: 5, 19, 20, 29, 41, 53, 59-63, 65, 66, 73, 76, 77, 80, 81, 83, 84, 86-88, 93, 98, 99, 101, 102, 105-108, 111, 112
Ant Spit: 98
Antwerp: 29
Arthur's Seat: 22
Astoria: 51

Backstairs Passage: 54
Ballarat: 80
Bancoora Beach: 101
Banks Strait: 64
Banool: 52
Barwon Heads: 14, 15, 36, 38, 42, 49, 56, 67, 68, 73, 75, 80, 92, 93, 98, 101, 106, 114, 115
Barrum River: 83
Barruppa: 43
Bass Strait: 5, 46, 62, 63, 66, 91, 111
Bay View Hotel: 48, 59
Bedford: 18
Bendigo: 91
Belfast: 43, 89, 90, 92
Bergen: 58
Blanket Bay: 94, 117
Bombay: 110
Boston: 109
Bluff: 7, 14, 93, 98, 101, 114
Breamlea: 106
Bream Creek: 13, 25, 56, 92, 93
Brisbane: 46, 112
Bridgewater Bay: 29, 57
Buckley's Cave: 35
Burnie: 83

Capetown: 5, 91
CAPES—
    Bridgewater: 10, 29, 32, 57, 96, 111
    Horn: 9, 51, 109
    Grant: 71
    Jaffa: 81
    Leeuwin: 64
    Nelson: 26, 45, 71, 76, 92
    Northumberland: 92
    Otway: 5, 7, 10-14, 18, 19, 22, 26, 29, 31, 33, 46, 48, 53-55, 58, 64-66, 70, 72, 73, 84, 86, 92, 94, 98, 104
    Good Hope: 21, 51, 110
    Patten: 52, 56, 75, 88, 101, 104, 107
    Schanck: 14, 15, 22, 36, 41, 88
    Wickham: 46
Canary Islands: 58
Castlemaine: 114
Chapple Vale: 45
Charente: 37

Charlemont Reef: 36
Childers Cove: 27
Christchurch: 117
Circular Head: 56, 74
Cliffy Island: 64
Cobden: 17, 45
Colac: 46, 52, 62
Corner Inlet: 74
Crayfish Bay: 94, 98
Curdies Inlet: 8, 10, 76, 110
Curdies River: 46

Darlots Creek: 111
Deal Island: 64
Demon's Bluff: 99
Dungeness: 16
Dunedin: 37, 58
Dundee: 46
Durban: 66

Erskine River: 72, 87, 102

Fitzroy River: 111
Falmouth: 107
Flaxman's Hill: 80
Flinders Island: 64, 92
Florida: 63, 64
Formby Reef: 67
Foochow: 33

Gallipoli: 52
Gellibrand River: 44, 116
Georgetown: 26
Geelong: 5, 7, 8, 13, 15, 17, 21, 23, 25, 37, 38, 55, 57, 73, 79, 80, 84, 85, 91, 94, 103, 107, 112, 113, 114, 116
Glenample: 15, 17, 18, 34, 95, 116
Gorman's Lane: 89
Godfrey River: 41, 93, 102
Gravesend: 16
Grey River: 59
Griffiths Island: 73, 75
Grimsby: 51
Guam: 31

Haley Reef: 73, 102
Hamilton: 90
Hamburg: 43
Henty Reef: 19, 31, 83
Hereford Reef: 48
High Cliff Beach: 17
Hobart: 37, 64, 69, 71
Hobsons Bay: 31, 69, 104, 109
Holdfast Bay: 92
Hong Kong: 28
Hopkins River: 48, 72, 85, 89

Indian Ocean: 64
Ingoldsby Reef: 48, 106

Jersey City: 46

139

LOCH ARD, wrecked near Port Campbell, 1878.

PERSONS

142

GENERAL

*William Ferrier, hero of wreck of LA BELLA
at Warrnambool, 1905.*